Hello My Beloved: God's Advice for Navigating the In-Between

Jerrica J. DeLaney

Hello My Beloved: God's Advice for Navigating the In-Between
Copyright © 2023 Jerrica J. DeLaney

To request permissions, contact the publisher at
publish@livingepistlespublishing.com.

ISBN: 979-8-9857898-3-6

First paperback edition August 2023.

Edited by Candice "Ordered Steps" Johnson/Bingeworthy Books
Cover art by Jerrica J. DeLaney
Photographs by Sarah Bridgeman Photography

Scriptures marked KJV are taken from the KING JAMES VERSION (KJV): KING JAMES VERSION, public domain.

Scriptures marked NIV are taken from the NEW INTERNATIONAL VERSION (NIV): Scripture taken from THE HOLY BIBLE, NEW INTERNATIONAL VERSION ®. Copyright© 1973, 1978, 1984, 2011 by Biblica, Inc.TM. Used by permission of Zondervan

Living Epistles Publishing

www.livingepistlespublishing.com

DEDICATION

To the 20-something and 30-something year old women who are
FINALLY surrendering this interesting season back to the One
who created it. May you trust God's guidance in your in between.

CONTENTS

ACKNOWLEDGMENTS

It could go without saying and be chalked up to being obvious; however, I wouldn't dare begin a book without thanking and acknowledging The Lord, Jesus Christ, whose words are what MADE this book. All glory and honor belong to You! I want to thank my mother, who spoke Jeremiah 29:11 over me from the time I was a small child. I want to thank my sister in Christ - NaTeesha, for pouring into me for over 10 years. You are truly My Elizabeth. I'd like to thank my sister Janae', who gave me three reasons to release this book: Jaelle, Skyy, and Heaven. Lastly, I'd like to thank my original writing partner, Mariama. The writing retreats we held on our apartment balconies and various parks have turned into two amazing testimonies that God is using. Thank you.

INTRODUCTION

Hello, Beloved of God!

I have always loved to read, and journaling, too. In my home, right now the bookshelves are lined with journals I've never finished. These unfinished notebooks and journals are chocked full of secrets, truths, lies I believed, and the wrongs God righted.

In 2017 I was living in my beautiful two-bedroom apartment and at a job I liked. I had just been diagnosed with a rare disease, and I felt like while good things were happening all around me, so were bad things. I was single and wanting a relationship to top things off. Amidst the feelings of brokenness, confusion, and loneliness were anger and so many questions. I began to ask God questions like, "How do I trust You for real when it seems like my world is falling apart?" "Father, how come no one ever showed me how true faith in life's challenges works?" The questions went on and on.

One day, completely depleted, hungry, and thirsty for God to respond, I sat at my desk with a notebook and pen. I cried, "Father, I repent for the attitude in which I asked you all these questions, but my heart really needs to know how to navigate these weird seasons of life. Will you teach me?" To my surprise, I felt the room get brighter and a coolness overcame my body. Within myself, I heard the words, "Hello my beloved." I didn't feel crazy and I knew it wasn't me talking because I do not say, "Hello My Beloved." It was God pressing in on my pain; responding to my cry. Word by word, sentence by sentence, paragraph by paragraph, God answered my questions. Soon, it was my daily ritual to inquire of the Lord and wait for His response. Every time I showed up with a sincere heart, so did He. One letter led to two, and two to 20. Twenty letters of His responses led to many more, but what was I to do with all He had said? I decided to make a bookmark of each and hand them out at random.

Thinking that my special bookmarks were all they would be, God said, "It's not a bookmark, it's a book." In true Jerrica fashion, I instead created a blog! I was so proud of this blog but after some time I asked the Lord what was next for these devotions, he responded, "Its not a bookmark or a blog, it's a book." When God told me the devotions were a book, doubt filled my heart. "*What do you mean a book Lord? I can barely finish a journal!*" But He repeated His instructions to me a few times, and I surrendered. So, here we have it - a combination of three things that make my heart sing the most: Jesus, journaling, and reading. All together in one book. A devotional journal, to be exact.

Even though I gave God my "yes" to writing this book, the thought of the over-saturated field I was jumping into flooded my mind. There were already so many books like the one I was about to publish out there, it scared me a bit. So, I sat on this project for some time. Eventually, God gently nudged me to move forward to complete the work. And I knew that my devotional journal wouldn't be like anyone else's. Why? Because it would be what God spoke to me.

This book is for the one who needs to know. *Needs to know what*, you may ask. The one who needs to know God.

You may need to know God exists, or that He loves you. You may need to know that He hears, or that He still speaks. You may need to know that He cares, corrects, and is concerned about you. This is for you. And it's for me, too. So pour that cup of tea, coffee, or glass of water – whichever you prefer. Then grab your Bible (and this journal), a highlighter and your favorite pen, and get ready to spend time with the One your soul longs for. He is waiting. He is here.

This journal has different sections, even one for guys. I want you to use that section to pray for and encourage the guys in your life. You can go through it in order, or skip around. Just read the devotion, then talk to God about what you're reading and learning. Hear and get to know the heart of Jesus through God's word as you chronicle your testimony.

Romans 10:11 (NKJV) says, "*For the scripture says, whoever believes on Him will not be ashamed.*" Believe that He is with you. *"Be still and know."* (Psalm 46:10 KJV).

HOW TO USE THIS BOOK

This book is a tool to serve you; in no way should it to be used without the Holy Bible.

Reading and responding to the prompts will make this journal work for you. The end of each devotion is followed by a few questions; I will encourage that as you respond and journal to the questions, listen for the voice of God even stronger.

Here are the journaling questions you'll use throughout the book:

1. What is the in-between of this letter? (Focus)
2. What is God saying about Himself? (Perspective)
3. What is God saying about me? (Perspective)
4. What advice is God giving me to live victoriously in the in-between? (Action)

When utilized correctly during your devotion time, the above questions will reveal:

- Where you're at, the in-between, the focus.

- The perspective of God's character that He wants you to maintain.
- The self-perspective He wants you to adopt.
- The action steps for you to walk victoriously through the in-between places of your life.

What is an In-Between?

An *in-between* is an "almost" area in your life. It's the place you are while on the path to where you want to be. It's a transitional place where character is developed, perspective is set, and action is required to successfully remain stable without fainting. During the in-between, the goal isn't simply to keep from fainting, it's to keep from fainting...joyfully.

"And let us not be weary in well doing: for in due season we shall reap, if we faint not."

Galatians 6:9 (KJV)

Our attitudes while navigating our *in-between* seasons determines the quality of the lessons we learn while we're in them. If I cry, moan and agonize my way through my singleness, by the time God releases me to marry the man of my dreams (should that happen), it wouldn't feel as sweet. Or say I complain about a challenging work environment instead of gracefully walking through it with God. When my dream job eventually shows itself and the same personality with a different face comes with it, I will not have built the character to love and rise above that circumstance. The goal again - no fainting, joyfully.

There's so much God wants to show us about Himself. To successfully navigate those in-between stages, we must maintain the proper perspective of who God is. We cannot look at Him as though He is a mere man. We must see the threads of His goodness and love permeating throughout our circumstance.

"For I am the Lord, I change not; therefore ye sons of Jacob are not consumed."

Malachi 3:6 (KJV)

"Jesus Christ the same yesterday, and today, and forever."

Hebrews 13:8 (KJV)

"Every good gift and every perfect gift is from above, and cometh down from the Father of lights, with whom is no variableness, neither shadow of turning."

James 1:17 (KJV)

Satan's goal is to get us to believe his lies about God's character. *"He is mean. He doesn't see you. He forgot about you. He doesn't think you're worthy. He's just going to change His mind."* Believing Satan's lies makes it impossible to trust God. We won't believe a word He says if we have not done away with the stinking thinking that would inhibit us from believing Holy God is good, especially during our in-between.

This book is to serve you and help redirect your mind to remembering the goodness of God. It guides you to the scriptures that support God's dynamic advice for navigating the in-between. Journal honestly with God. Seek Him and you will find Him. When you're finished, you will look back on this journal and thank God for revealing Himself, highlighting His instruction for you, and giving you victory in your in-between!

What in-between am I in right now?

_____

_____

_____

_____

_____

_____

What does not fainting - *joyfully*, look like for me right now?

_____

_____

_____

_____

_____

_____

Enjoy this journey through the in-between!

PART 1

Our 20s are a very interesting time in life. We think we're grown, but we're not. We think we have a plan, but if we're honest with ourselves, more often than not, we don't. Our 20s are the years where we can try new things, experiment, and totally blow whatever our "it" is, and people will extend us grace because we're so young.

My twenties were somewhat of a blur. I thought I had a plan: finish college, get a great job, make lots of money, get married and have some babies. Well, God had other plans. I did indeed finish college. I attended a great school for undergrad, then a Big 10 university for graduate school. Afterwards, I landed a good paying job for a girl fresh out of grad school in the field of social work. I was on my own, doing what was socially expected of me. Time was ticking; no man had swooped me off the market, thus, no children actualized from my dreams. Okay, so life wasn't going exactly how I planned, and I was struggling. Can you relate?

In my wonderful fresh-out-of-school job, I was met with challenges and lessons that hurt, bad. My character was tried, health issues humbled me, and being the mature (but not quite there yet) Christian I was, I kicked and screamed the entire way through.

I sought the advice of women I looked up to, and they gave it in abundance! Maybe a little too much. One thing that started to occur was that those well-meaning women (some who genuinely cared for my wellbeing), overwhelmed me with such an abundance of advice, their opinions started drowning out the voice of God in my life.

The Backstory

I grew up in the church. I jokingly tell people that I was born in the pew. I learned about God at a very young age, and as I grew, I eventually learned to love Him. I accepted Jesus Christ as my Lord and Savior on October 31, 1999; on December 19th that same year, I was baptized and launched straight into holy honeymoon bliss! Then, life happened. My world was rocked; all of my accomplishments came at a price. Trying to maintain an air of perfection resulted in my wearing a mask to hide depression, low self-esteem, and self-hatred. All the while, God had a hold on me. Through various trials, I cried out to Him. He answered and comforted me. I sat for hours in His presence, read His Word and sought to understand His heart for me. Now let me say, I was in no way perfect - I had secret sins piled a mile high. (I'll testify about my deliverance in another book). As you read, you may be thinking, *What is she talking about, sitting for hours in His presence?* It's simple: I opened the Holy Bible, God's Word to help us get to know and navigate life with and through Him. I silenced all the noise around me (cell phone, television, social media), and sat quietly in prayer to heal and rest from my burdens.

Around this time, I began thinking about mentorship. I was pressed to find mentors and women to pour truth into me. Mentorship itself isn't bad; however, we must be led by Holy Spirit, our Helper to decipher through the voices; to be able to discern sheep from wolves. I clung to whomever would shepherd me through womanhood, which seemed like a great idea, until it wasn't. Eventually, the voices of the women around me grew louder than God's. When I'd try to spread my wings a bit and fly, some - not all of the women, tried molding me into being their protégé, rather than the woman God destined me to be.

The Letters

One day while sitting in my apartment office, I burst into crocodile tears before The Lord, screaming and crying for help. I needed to hear what HE had to say about my life and the direction it was going. I needed Him to eliminate the bad advice I received, highlight the good, and fill in the gaps with the truth of His Word.

Side note, sisters: Never be afraid to ugly cry before Jesus. He is not scared of your meltdown, but remember, we are talking to our Holy God. So, keep the meltdown short and sweet. You are before a King and Father, to be reverenced and trusted.

As I wept at my desk, I spotted a piece of paper and a pen in front of my computer. I calmed down, picked up my pen, and began to write **Hello, My Beloved...**

I was writing at what felt like the speed of light, yet evenly paced out. I may have been hearing faster than I wrote. It wasn't me writing of myself, though. Now pause right here and hear me out. I wasn't on a spooky, spiritual type of flow; however, it was God speaking to my spirit, answering questions and giving advice on things I hadn't verbally asked. He was answering and speaking to the deep ponderings of my heart. The things He spoke weren't different than what His Word says in the Bible, but it was like He highlighted them just for me. He made His words come alive in my heart! I want to share with you what I learned. This book is comprised of the letters God wrote me when I was at my lowest, trying to navigate between the place I was at, and the place I wanted to be. These letters taught me how to behave and grow as a follower of Jesus Christ, constantly refining my character and compelling me to mature in Him. I believe these letters will bless you too. Here are the lessons from my 20s.

LESSONS FROM MY 20S

From: God
A Note on Focus

Hello My Beloved,

Fight for your focus. There are many things that will try to distract you from hearing Me, and they will be victorious if you do not fight for your focus.

What you give your eye to, you give your ear to, and what you give your ear to, you give your heart to. If you **have your eyes set** on Jesus, you **converse** with Him. Once you converse with Him, you take **interest** in Him. Once you take interest, you invest intimacy with Him - **intimacy** being to give significant time, attention, and focus to. Once you are intimate with the object of your desire - Jesus, your heart opens to **receive seed** (wisdom, word, instruction, suggestion) from Him. Once you receive the seed, it grows and **bears fruit**.

The same is true with distractions. Once you take your focus off Jesus to entertain distractions, you start to **converse** with them. For example, you're scrolling through social media, and see your friend just got engaged. You're so happy for them…until you start feeling sad because you're still single. **PAUSE**. You have just taken your eyes off of Jesus, who gives you contentment and joy, to hold a conversation with your distraction instead. Next, you type your ex's name in the search box to see how they're doing, find out they're in a new relationship, and sink a bit more. **PAUSE.** You have just become **interested** in the distraction. Now, you start wondering what's wrong with you, why you weren't good enough, and when the person for you will surface. In your misery, you post your own status in response. **PAUSE.** You have now gotten **intimate** with the distraction. You've meditated on it, let it roll over and over in your mind, and opened your heart to **receive the seed** from it: lies about your identity, blows to your esteem and contentment, doubt about God's character and how He cares care for you. Finally, you leave your heart on the scathing status you post. *Back then they didn't want me, now I'm hot, they all on me. You're going to miss me when I'm gone. Funny how they don't want you, and the next be an almost clone of you.* The **fruit** of your distraction from Jesus Christ always leads to pride and self-dependence. Beloved, this is not how I designed your focus to be!

You cannot spell heart without hear, nor hear without ear. Give Me your ear, and I will tell you good and wonderful things that you have never imagined. Where your heart is, your treasure is. Am I your treasure? Am I the object of your desire? Is your focus on Me? If it is not, **SHIFT YOUR FOCUS, DO IT BY FORCE.** Let your eyes find My Word, and your ears hear My voice. Focus on ME.

> 2 Set your affection on things above, not on things on the earth.
> Colossians 3:2 (KJV)

> Let thine eyes look right on, and let thine eyelids look straight before thee.
> Proverbs 4:25 (KJV)

> For they that are after the flesh do mind the things of the flesh; but they that are after the Spirit the things of the Spirit.
>
> Romans 8:5 (KJV)

> For where your treasure is, there will your heart be also.
> Matthew 6:21 (KJV)

> **My sheep** hear **my** voice, and I know them, and they follow

me:
John 10:27 (KJV)

Love, Abba Father

Respond

What is the in-between of this letter? (Focus)

_____

_____

_____

_____

_____

_____

What is God saying about Himself? (Perspective)

_____

_____

_____

_____

_____

_____

What is God saying about me? (Perspective)

_____

_____

_____

_____

_____

_____

What advice is God giving me to live victoriously in this in-between? (Action)

_____

_____

_____

_____

_____

_____

From: God
To: The One Who Needs to Unpack the Box

Hello My Beloved,

I love you and I love when you come to Me with everything - all your cares, concerns, hurts, joy, and desires. However, there is one thing I have against you...your sharp demands of Me. As Holy God and Your Father, I am in control and able to handle the who, what, where, when, why, and how of your life. Really, I am.

You are seeking identity and purpose, ministry and mission, direction and clarity, but there is a better way to ask than the way in which you have been asking Me for it. "GOD, just tell me what I am supposed to do!" "GOD, just tell me what my purpose is, so I can please you!" "GOD, just be my genie and give me everything I want when I want it!" This is how I hear you.

Beloved, just unpack the box. I have a daughter who just moved into the new dwelling I led her to. She unpacked and set in order every room, except one. She prepared her bedroom so she could rest, and converted the second bedroom into an office to work and spend time with Me. She even prepared the living and dining rooms to entertain others. The one space she did not prepare? The place where she was to eat...*her kitchen*. For a week, she needed two things: utensils to cook and eat with, and cups to drink from. For days, she shuffled back and forth past unopened boxes in the kitchen. "What if they're all down in the basement?" she asked herself. "Ugh, I am not going down there to sift through all those boxes anytime soon." Not once had it dawned on her to open the boxes within her reach.

One day, she decided she was tired of looking at the boxes, and opened one. Inside, she found the things she needed to keep, store, give away, or throw away. She would not have made that discovery had she not opened that box. She found exactly what she was looking for as she kept opening boxes! Even her cups and utensils were ready to use, which she would've known sooner if she had just opened the box.

Beloved, the things you have been asking and pleading for, sometimes even demanding from Me, are all in the box: My Word. And it is not tucked away in storage, it is within your reach. So all you need to do, is open the box. And even if you do have My truth stored away, do you not find it valuable enough to seek out and sift through? You know you don't have but need it, because you've used it before. You brought it to the new place I've brought you. The only difference between use and loss, is failing to open the box. Want identity, purpose, direction, mission, ministry, answers, and everything you need? Open the box.

"According as his divine power hath given unto us all things that *pertain* unto life and godliness, through the knowledge of him that hath called us to glory and virtue."
2 Peter 1:3 (KJV)

Love, Abba Father

Respond

What is the in-between of this letter? (Focus)

_____

_____

_____

_____

_____

_____

What is God saying about Himself? (Perspective)

_____

_____

_____

_____

_____

_____

What is God saying about me? (Perspective)

_____

_____

_____

_____

_____

_____

What advice is God giving me to live victoriously in this in-between? (Action)

_____

_____

_____

_____

_____

_____

From: God
To: The One Who Doesn't Know Where to Lean

Hello My Beloved,

I want to share with you a story about a daughter who did not know where to lean. In one case, she leaned in the right direction, and in another, she leaned in the wrong direction. Are you in a spot where you do not know what direction to lean in times of trouble? Look at this story, and hear My voice through it:

There was a young professional named Janell. She worked at a top university, making a generous salary for an entry level position in her field, and getting great benefits. Janell had a difficult supervisor she was under. He was quite the antagonist. She equated him to sandpaper. He would irritate, challenge, and agitate this blooming young professional.

At her wits end, Janell, would pray fervently about her sandpaper supervisor. "Lord, I don't care if I get any glory for the work I do, but for Your name's sake, shut Him up and shut his attacks down! For Your glory alone God! In Jesus' name, Amen." Janell continued to pray secretly and excelled. This was her pattern—pray, excel, give God glory. Pray, excel, give God glory.

When Janell came to the decision to quit her job and follow Jesus further on her adventure to a new job and relocation, she was prepared. Why? Because she leaned on Jesus. He used her sandpaper supervisor to smooth out some crooks that would have snagged and left her unprepared for the next season. Janell followed Jesus boldly and courageously, despite the slack she got for her decision. God was providing and giving her all she needed, including a path to her dream job.

Janell now had an oily supervisor. He slid through his position and the slickness rubbed off on Janell. She complained that she could not get a grip on things, and had worked hard just to spin her wheels and get nowhere. "I know my previous job and elite education prepared me for this. God, I thought you had me in this." Janell quickly burned out and was full of resentment towards her oily boss. Instead of praying, she complained.

Janell did pray; however, that God would present the oily supervisor with an offer he could not deny - a new job. A year and a half later, God did it! Janell was happy! But when the opportunity for advancement came, she was not fully prepared, because for that year and a half instead of leaning on Jesus as she did in the previous season, she leaned on herself, and it showed. She got by, but barely.

But God is shaping and molding Janell as she realigned herself and meditates on this valuable lesson.

I am crying out to you Beloved, to LEAN ON ME. I will hold and keep you if you allow Me to. I have you in the palm of my hand. So, LEAN IN.

"Trust in the Lord with all thine heart; and lean not unto thine own understanding. In all thy ways acknowledge him, and he shall direct thy paths."
Proverbs 3:5-6 (KJV)

"The steps of a good man are ordered by the Lord: and he delighteth in his way."
Psalm 37:23 (KJV)

"If any of you lack wisdom, let him ask of God, that giveth to all men liberally, and upbraideth not; and it shall be given him."
James 1:5 (KJV)

Beloved, lean into Me. You will find all the direction, strength, clarity, peace, and preparation when you do.

Love, Abba Father
Respond

What is the in-between of this letter? (Focus)

_____
_____
_____
_____
_____
_____
_____

What is God saying about Himself? (Perspective)

_____

_____

_____

_____

_____

_____

What is God saying about me? (Perspective)

_____

_____

_____

_____

_____

_____

What advice is God giving me to live victoriously in this in-between? (Action)

_____

_____

_____

_____

_____

_____

From: God
To: The One Getting Weary In Well Doing

Hello My Beloved,

I see you. I see you fighting and contending for the faith, and standing up for righteousness and justice with a broken heart for the things that break My heart. I see your will bent in submission towards My will, for My use and pleasure.

I see you wondering where I am, and why I am seemingly moving so slow. I am not mad at you for feeling the way you do, but like Job, do not curse me. I have double joy, double rest, double victory, and restoration in store for you as you stand and fight.

I see you clothed with My full armor. I see your loins girded with the belt of truth and you wearing the breastplate of righteousness. I see you wearing the preparation of the gospel of peace as your sandals and holding up the shield of faith. I see your mind protected with the helmet of salvation, and you bearing up the Sword of the Spirit, My Word. And yes, I hear the mighty weapon of prayer on your lips. I cannot ignore the sweet-smelling incense of your words in My nostrils, engaging My attention and sending angels into flight to fight spiritually for you.

As My Son was beloved, I see you being tempted in the wilderness and tried on every side and yet standing on the truth of scripture! Just as I sent ministering angels to My Son when He victoriously endured temptation, beloved I will send them to you before you begin your public ministry.

Each experience I allow shapes and molds you more and more into the image of My Son. So, when they see you, they see Him. Beloved, your agitators do not despise you, they despise Me! But if you endure this persecution and do not faint or bow to the enemy, you will be blessed! I am holding you up with My righteous right hand, so STAND!

And let us not be weary in well doing: for in due season we shall reap, if we faint not.
Galatians 6:9 (KJV)

Blessed are they which are persecuted for righteousness' sake: for theirs is the Kingdom of Heaven.

Matthew 5:10 (KJV)

Blessed are ye, when men shall revile you, and persecute you, and shall say all manner of evil against you falsely, for My sake.
Matthew 5:11 (KJV)

If ye be reproached for the name of Christ, happy are ye; for the spirit of glory and of God resteth upon you: on their part He is evil spoken of, but on your part He is glorified.

1 Peter 4:14 (KJV)

They shall bear thee up in their hands, lest thou dash thy foot against a stone.
Psalm 91:12 (KJV)

Fear thou not; for I am with thee: be not dismayed; for I am thy God: I will strengthen thee; yea, I will help thee; yea, I will uphold thee with the right hand of my righteousness.
Isaiah 41:10 (KJV)

But they that wait upon the LORD shall renew their strength; they shall mount up with wings as eagles; they shall run, and not be weary; and they shall walk, and not faint.
Isaiah 40:31 (KJV)

You will not be worn down! I see you, My beloved. Stand, and faint NOT!

Love, Abba Father

Respond

What is the in-between of this letter? (Focus)

_____
_____
_____
_____
_____

What is God saying about Himself? (Perspective)

_____
_____
_____
_____
_____

What is God saying about me? (Perspective)

_____
_____
_____
_____
_____

What advice is God giving me to live victoriously in this in-between?
(Action)

_____
_____
_____
_____
_____

From: God

A Note on Faith

Hello My Beloved,

I see you. You study and read My Word, even memorize My scriptures. I love it because you learn My voice.

I am going to submit to you; however, a note on your proper perception of My Word. I know you have heard many sermons about faith, but by grace I say, you've gotten it partially right, and partially wrong.

"Now faith is the substance of things hoped for, the evidence
of things not seen."
-Hebrews 11:1 (KJV)

You will not get more correct than this. You have the knowledge of the verse down, but the understanding is where we will do some work.

The first verse below is followed by other verses which explain it; scripture interprets scripture. Each explains what faith does. Faith does not spin around three times, slap its neighbor, or put an olive oil drenched cloth under its pillow. Observe through the Heroes of Faith outlined in Hebrews 11, on what faith really does, then you can determine whether or not you exercise faith in the various situations of life.

³ Through faith we understand that the worlds were framed by the word of God, so that things which are seen were not made of things which do appear.
⁴ By faith Abel offered unto God a more excellent sacrifice than Cain, by which he obtained witness that he was righteous, God testifying of his gifts: and by it he being dead yet speaketh.
⁵ By faith Enoch was translated that he should not see death; and was not found, because God had translated him: for before his translation he had this testimony, that he pleased God. ⁷ By faith Noah, being warned of God of things not seen as yet, moved with

fear, prepared an ark to the saving of his house; by the which he condemned the world, and became heir of the righteousness which is by faith.

8 By faith Abraham, when he was called to go out into a place which he should after receive for an inheritance, obeyed; and he went out, not knowing whither he went.

9 By faith he sojourned in the land of promise, as in a strange country, dwelling in tabernacles with Isaac and Jacob, the heirs with him of the same promise:

10 For he looked for a city which hath foundations, whose builder and maker is God.

11 Through faith also Sara herself received strength to conceive seed, and was delivered of a child when she was past age, because she judged him faithful who had promised.

Hebrews 11:3-5, 7-11 (KJV)

Hero	Verse	Faith Action
God	3	Framed
Abel	4	Offered
Enoch	5	Testified
Noah	7	Prepared
Abraham	8	Obeyed
Abraham	9-10	Sojourned
Sarah	11	Received

The last verse I want to share is:

6 But without faith it is impossible to please him: for he that cometh to God must believe that he is, and that he is a rewarder of them that diligently seek him.

Hebrews 11:6 (KJV)

Beloved, does your faith: frame, offer, testify, prepare, obey, sojourn, receive, believe, and seek? Meditate on this word. Exercise it. Let it transform your thinking and actions. Have REAL faith. I'll help you, if you allow Me to.

Love, Abba Father

Respond

What is the in-between of this letter? (Focus)

_____

_____

_____

_____

_____

_____

What is God saying about Himself? (Perspective)

_____

_____

_____

_____

_____

_____

What is God saying about me? (Perspective)

_____

_____

_____

_____

_____

_____

What advice is God giving me to live victoriously in this in-between? (Action)

_____

_____

_____

_____

_____

_____

_____

From: God
A Note on Joy

Hello My Beloved,

Sustained joy equals sustained gaze. Gaze on what, you may ask? Gaze set on Me, your God, your Lover. Sustained means continuing for an extended period or without interruption. If you desire sustained joy in your heart no matter the circumstance, you must keep your gaze sustained - without interruption on Me. It will be the difference between walking on water and succumbing to the storms life throws at you.

Take Peter for an example in Matthew 14:22-31(NIV):

22 Immediately, Jesus made the disciples get into the boat and go on ahead of him to the other side, while he dismissed the crowd. 23 After he had dismissed them, he went up on a mountainside by himself to pray. Later that night, he was there alone, 24 and the boat was already a considerable distance from land, buffeted by the waves because the wind was against it.

25 Shortly before dawn Jesus went out to them, walking on the lake. 26 When the disciples saw him walking on the lake, they were terrified. "It's a ghost," they said, and cried out in fear.

27 But Jesus immediately said to them: "Take courage! It is I. Don't be afraid."

28 "Lord, if it's you," Peter replied, "tell me to come to you on the water."

29 "Come," he said.

Then Peter got down out of the boat, walked on the water and came toward Jesus. 30 But when he saw the wind, he was afraid and, beginning to sink, cried out, "Lord, save me!"

31 Immediately Jesus reached out his hand and caught him. "You of little faith," he said, "why did you doubt?"

Broken gaze = broken joy. When Peter broke gaze from My Son, he sank. The joy of sustained gaze can cause you to walk into situations that could kill you and cause you to lose your mind. But if you fix your eyes on Jesus, you will walk right into His presence, where there is fullness of joy forevermore.

The scripture is seeped with the connection between joy and

vision:

1 Blessed is the man that walketh not in the counsel of the ungodly, nor standeth in the way of sinners, nor sitteth in the seat of the scornful.

2 But his delight is in the law of the Lord; and in his law doth he meditate day and night.

3 And he shall be like a tree planted by the rivers of water, that bringeth forth his fruit in his season; his leaf also shall not wither; and whatsoever he doeth shall prosper.

Psalm 1:1-3 (KJV)

8 I have set the Lord always before me: because he is at my right hand, I shall not be moved.

9 Therefore my heart is glad, and my glory rejoiceth: my flesh also shall rest in hope.

10 For thou wilt not leave my soul in hell; neither wilt thou suffer thine Holy One to see corruption.

11 Thou wilt shew me the path of life: in thy presence is fulness of joy; at thy right hand there are pleasures for evermore.

Psalm 16:8-11 (KJV)

8 The statutes of the Lord are right, **rejoicing the heart**: the commandment of the Lord is pure, **enlightening the eyes.**

Psalm 19:8 (KJV)

5 They looked unto him, and were lightened: and their faces were not ashamed.

Psalm 34:5 (KJV)

Beloved, joy comes with many benefits. Look at the outcome of joy in James 1:2-4 (KJV):

2 My brethren, count it all joy when ye fall into divers temptations;

3 Knowing this, that the trying of your faith worketh patience.

4 But let patience have her perfect work, that ye may be perfect and entire, wanting nothing.

My Son was an example of sustained gaze, equaling sustained joy in Hebrews 12:1-2 (KJV):

12 Wherefore seeing we also are compassed about with so great a cloud of witnesses, let us lay aside every weight, and the sin which doth so easily beset us, and let us run with patience the race that is set before us,

2 Looking unto Jesus the author and finisher of our faith; who for the joy that was set before him endured the cross, despising the shame, and is set down at the right hand of the throne of God.

His gaze was set on the hope of you running to Him, and accepting His sacrificial love for you. What do you see? Do you see Me in and through all of your visions, thoughts, dreams and desires? Yes, I know the winds and waves are present and real, but where is your gaze sustained?

The importance of joy can be found in Proverbs 17:22 (KJV):

22 A merry heart doeth good like a medicine: but a broken spirit drieth the bones.

A joyful heart is medicine for you and others. Another and an even richer reason for joy is found in the beginning words of Hebrews 12:1 (KJV) where it says, "Wherefore seeing we also are compassed about with so great a cloud of witnesses." The lost are not going to want a God whose followers are joyless.

Beloved, you have the best reason to be joyful: ME. Sustained gaze=sustained joy. Where is your gaze set?

Love, Abba Father

Respond

What is the in-between of this letter? (Focus)

_____
_____
_____
_____
_____
_____

What is God saying about Himself? (Perspective)

_____
_____
_____
_____
_____
_____

What is God saying about me? (Perspective)

_____
_____
_____
_____
_____
_____

What advice is God giving me to live victoriously in this in-between? (Action)

_____
_____
_____
_____
_____
_____

From: God
To: The One I'm Training in Isolation

Hello My Beloved,

I know you have been under a bit of pressure in this season. You have been charging forward with weak hands and a willing heart into the things I have for you. You are holding onto the promise I made, and the Word I spoke over your life. I see you.

I know you have been uncomfortable in isolation, and that you really want someone to ride this season out with you, but Beloved, I cannot allow that right now. I will always send you encouragement and refreshing when you need it most. I will send the hug, the kiss, the person to listen when you need it most. But I will allow this isolation for a moment. It is in your solitude that I am training you. Everyone cannot see what I am doing. I do not want anyone or anything taking away your attention from Me. Yes, your phone will be dry, and no one will call or text you. I am training you during this isolation.

You are not alone. There are a many of My beloved that I have trained in isolation. Look at My servant David, and how he was a shepherd for many years, fighting bears and predators off the sheep. I was preparing him to be a mighty warrior and shepherd of my people.

"Thy servant slew both the lion and the bear: and this uncircumcised Philistine shall be as one of them, seeing he hath defied the armies of the living God."
1 Samuel 17:36 (KJV)

Look at My servant Moses, who went through the wilderness for 40 years before I led him back to Egypt to free my people. He had to lead them through the wilderness for 40 years to get to the Promised Land.

Beloved, what you do in secret will be rewarded openly. Keep praying in secret. Keep giving in secret. Keep denying yourself in secret. I will reward you openly. You think you have been shadowboxing in the spirit for naught; however, you are preparing to stand against the enemy of God and win the greatest battle in history as My warrior.

I am training you in secret to be an articulate, effective communicator with Me because in due season, you will be communicating My truths to many publicly. I am training you to hear My voice in isolation because out in the open, you will say what I said. I am training you to study and get understanding of My Word in private, because you will teach My principles in public to many. I am training you to forgive in secret, because I will make your enemies your footstool openly; there is no space in My miracles for pride, arrogance, and believing you earned anything. Love covers a multitude of sin and forgiveness training will reveal that.

So just know Beloved, I am with you. I am your Teacher. I am your example. Look at my Son, as He trained in isolation to submit to My will and not His own. He is now the Savior of the world, Ruler, and King throughout all eternity. Beautiful things come from training in isolation.

For who hath despised the day of small things? For they shall rejoice and shall see the plummet in the hand of Zerubbabel *with* those seven; they *are* the eyes of the LORD, which run to and fro through the whole earth.
Zechariah 4:10 (KJV)

Love, Abba Father

Respond

What is the in-between of this letter? (Focus)

What is God saying about Himself? (Perspective)

_____
_____
_____
_____
_____
_____

What is God saying about me? (Perspective)

_____
_____
_____
_____
_____

What advice is God giving me to live victoriously in this in-between? (Action)

_____
_____
_____
_____
_____
_____

From: God
A Note on Surviving the Weight of Wait

My Beloved,

> "Hope deferred maketh the heart sick."
> Proverbs 13: 12 (KJV)

Waiting is one of the most challenging things I will ask you to do. It is right on par with "Trust Me." I realize that waiting carries a weight to it, and sometimes that weight zaps your strength. But Beloved, I would not introduce a wait that I could not restore you from.

> Even youths grow tired and weary,
> and young men stumble and fall;
> 31 but those who hope in the Lord
> will renew their strength.
> They will soar on wings like eagles;
> they will run and not grow weary,
> they will walk and not be faint.
> Isaiah 40:30-31 (NIV)

Beloved, I hear your heart and see your pain. I hear you questioning when, why, how long, and is it time yet. I hear you…but now, I need you to hear Me.

There is something I am trying to build in you and it takes time. I am trying to build patience.

"2 My brethren, count it all joy when ye fall into divers temptations;

3 Knowing this, that **the trying of your faith worketh patience.**

4 But **let patience have her perfect work, that ye may be perfect and entire, wanting nothing."**

James 1:2-4 (KJV)

"3 **His divine power has given us everything we need for a godly life** through our knowledge of him who called us by his own glory and goodness. 4 Through these he has given us his very great and precious promises, so that through them you may participate in the divine nature, having escaped the corruption in the world caused by evil desires.

5 For this very reason, make every effort to add to your faith goodness; and to goodness, knowledge; 6 and to knowledge, self-control; and to self-control, **perseverance**; and to perseverance, godliness; 7 and to godliness, mutual affection; and to mutual affection, love. 8 **For if you possess these qualities in increasing measure, they will keep you from being ineffective and unproductive in your knowledge of our Lord Jesus Christ.**"

2 Peter 1:3-8 (NIV)

Beloved, I need you to look like and respond like Me in this evil world. I need you to be on mission about my mission. I need to wring out the desires in your heart that do not match Mine, or that have grown so large, they overshadow the desire you were created to be fulfilled by, and that is Me.

Beloved, if I did heal, deliver, present the job opportunity, present your husband, allow the baby to form, or did whatever your "it" is NOW, ask yourself, **"Would the Giver of the gift still have the throne of my heart if I got the gift now?"** One thing that the weight of wait encourages is **humility and gratitude**. These are the muscles you build when you wait on Me and trust Me. And patience? Patience is like the heart. If your patience is strong, humility and gratitude can lift any weight that I ask you to wait for. Beloved, I see you and do not forget your effort.

"God is not unjust; he will not forget your work and the love you have shown him as you have helped his people and continue to help them."

Hebrews 6:10 (NIV)

Bless others while you wait! Sing praise unto Me as you wait! Learn of Me while you wait! And one day Beloved, the transfer of My desires for you into your heart will be so full and complete, you will begin to help others bear the weight of wait, and then the weight will not seem so bad. You will be working your wait so well, that when the reward meets you, you will be whole, complete, and lacking nothing.

Remain, Beloved! I am helping you lift the weight of wait!

"But *when* the desire cometh, *it is* a tree of life."
Proverbs 13:12b (KJV)

Love, Abba Father

Respond

What is the in-between of this letter? (Focus)

_____

_____

_____

_____

_____

_____

What is God saying about Himself? (Perspective)

_____

_____

_____

_____

_____

_____

What is God saying about me? (Perspective)

_____

_____

_____

_____

_____

_____

What advice is God giving me to live victoriously in this in-between? (Action)

_____

_____

_____

_____

_____

_____

From: God
A Matter of Principle

Hello My Beloved,

Often, you are looking for the formula or the strategy for how to get the optimal results in a given situation. What if I told you that you already have access to them, but have decided not to use them? What if I told you that you have the keys to unlock everything I have for you, requests that I could not ignore, but you'd have to die to get them? Would you be all in, or would you bail on our relationship?

I have a set of principles that will build My character in you, if you follow them. Does this mean that you will walk through life without a problem in the world? Quite the contrary. But you will bring Me most glory and bear witness to Me if you follow what I instruct you to do. My Son gave a sermon on the top of a mountain, and it is the longest recorded dialogue that you have of Him. He is sharing My heart and will for you, so I want you to dig in and do as I instruct. You may not get it right the first time, but that's where dying to your ways and your flesh comes into play. If you want My best for yourself and your situation, you have to put My principles to work in your life.

See the principles recorded throughout Matthew 5-7 (NIV):

Let your light shine so men can see your good works and glorify your Father who is in heaven.

Your righteousness must exceed that of the scribes and Pharisees if you want to get into heaven.

Anyone angry with their brother or sister will be subject to judgement—leave your gift at the altar, get it right with them, then come back to offer it to God.

Do not commit adultery—watch your eyes—cut off anything that is going to cause you to sin in the physical and in your heart.

No divorce except for fornication—any man that marries a

divorced woman is committing adultery.

Do not make vows—let your "yes" be "yes" and your "no" be "no"—anything else is evil.

Do not resist an evil person—turn the other cheek—if someone ask you to go a mile with them, go two—if someone ask to borrow, give it to them.

Love your enemies—pray for those who persecute you.

Give secretly—don't show off for others how you give—secret service, public reward.

Do not pray in vain with repetitions and many words—pray like Jesus—secret prayer, open reward.

Put oil on your head and wash your face when fasting—everyone shouldn't know you're fasting—secret sacrifice, public reward.

Don't store up treasure on earth, store it up in heaven. Your treasure is where your heart is.

Don't worry about what you will eat or drink, wear or live—seek first God and His Kingdom and everything you need will come to you.

You'll be judged the same way you judge others—take the beam out your eye before you get the speck out your brother's eye.

Ask, seek, and knock—keep asking, seeking, and knocking—do to others what you want done to you.

The way to heaven is narrow, the way to hell is broad—make sure you work to find the unpopular route to life.

Watch out for false prophets—check their fruit.

Only those who do My Father's will enter into heaven.

Fools build their lives on the temporary—wise men build it on the Rock, Jesus—hear and DO, not just hear.

So you see My Beloved, when I instruct you in a way and you take it, you look more like Me, please and bring glory to Me, and you bear witness to Me in a dying world. They see that you look like Me, then they become attracted to Me through you. Obedience to principles is the hard and rewarding work that comes only through love and submission to Me. Follow Me.

Love, Abba Father

Respond

What is the in-between of this letter? (Focus)

_____

_____

_____

_____

_____

_____

What is God saying about Himself? (Perspective)

_____

_____

_____

_____

_____

_____

What is God saying about me? (Perspective)

_____

_____

_____

_____

_____

_____

What advice is God giving me to live victoriously in this in-between? (Action)

_____

_____

_____

_____

_____

_____

From: God
To: The Child Who Always Has Something to Say

Oh My Beloved,

I love you. I love you so very much, but I really need you to be quiet.

When and if you come into My presence, you have so much to say. I love to hear your voice and I want you to cast all your cares on Me, but you my beloved, forget my My personhood. You forget that part of the art of conversation is listening. I have things I want to say to you. There are also times when I just want you to take in My presence, silently.

"Now when they saw the boldness of Peter and John, and perceived that they were unlearned and ignorant men, they marveled; and they took knowledge of them, that they had been with Jesus."
Acts 4:13 (KJV)

Part of being with Me is being quiet, and being taught. To be My disciple means being My student, and posturing your heart to learn and hear. I am after your heart. Interestingly enough, you cannot spell the word "heart" without the word "hear," and you cannot spell "hear" without the word "ear." I want your heart, so give Me your ear. Listen to Me. Intimate time listening to Me privately will publicly show that you have been in My presence. Beloved, you cannot effectively hear and receive while you are talking.

"Be not rash with thy mouth, and let not thine heart be hasty to utter anything before God: for God is in heaven, and thou upon earth: therefore let thy words be few."
Ecclesiastes 5:2 (KJV)

I am Holy God, and you are my beloved; however, let your words in My presence be few. I am the God who stores every tear you cry. I know the depths of your heart, because I created it. I know you. I want to converse with you and hear what you have to say, but I really need you to come to Me in the proper posture first. What is that posture? Is it sitting, kneeling, laid prostrate? It is a quieted heart, no matter how heavy, and a listening ear. It is worship out of a pure place. It is humility and a killing of pride and demand of Me. It is agreement with who I am, who you are and how I feel about you. Save your words for worship, and wait. Then petition. But first comes worship.

I know silence can be unnerving and uncomfortable. Just wait. Quiet yourself and expect Me to show up. You'll find that I've already been there waiting for you. Also, stop comparing how the next person *got to Me*, just focus on YOU and Me. I do not speak to everyone the same way. Focus on Me. I have something to say. Be available, and be quiet. And if you must speak, start with thanksgiving and worship.

[17] Pray without ceasing.
[18] In everything give thanks: for this is the will of God in Christ Jesus concerning you.
[19] Quench not the Spirit.
1 Thessalonians 5:17-19 (KJV)

Do not quench My Spirit. I love you. I want to hear you. I have something to say, but I really need you to be quiet.

Love, Abba Father

Respond

What is the in-between of this letter? (Focus)

_____
_____
_____
_____
_____
_____

What is God saying about Himself? (Perspective)

_____
_____
_____
_____
_____
_____

What is God saying about me? (Perspective)

_____
_____
_____
_____
_____
_____

What advice is God giving me to live victoriously in this in between? (Action)

_____
_____
_____
_____
_____
_____

From: God
To: The Last Pick

Hello My Beloved,

When I look on you, I smile. Having you as My child brings My heart so much joy. You truly do make Me proud.

Here you are, watching everyone around you be "blessed," and you are next in line. I know you feel that you are the last pick, but I have something to say about that:

"So the last shall be first, and the first last: for many be called, but few chosen."
Matthew 20:16 (KJV)

In My Kingdom, the way up is down. I love the lowly. I value the meek. I like the last pick. All who are called by Me are blessed, but there is something special about the last pick.

The last pick gets to see the full testimony of My goodness, and how time and time again, I have proven Myself mighty.

The last pick has a front row view of the lessons of those who were picked before them. They're the ones who get to observe their predecessors' trials and triumphs, and have the opportunity to adjust their behavior and posture their hearts accordingly.

The last pick gets the most time in anticipation of Me. When they are finally picked and called upon, they are closest to the field, because the dugout is full. They go from last picked, to first up to bat. They get first crack at the enemy. They reign with Me.

All of My picks are blessed, but there is a special place in My heart for the last. You see Beloved, the last have believed, even when they could not see and I honor that.

"Wherein ye greatly rejoice, though now for a season, if need be, ye are in heaviness through manifold temptations:
7 That the trial of your faith, being much more precious than of

gold that perisheth, though it be tried with fire, might be found unto praise and honour and glory at the appearing of Jesus Christ:

⁸ Whom having not seen, ye love; in whom, though now ye see him not, yet believing, ye rejoice with joy unspeakable and full of glory:

⁹ Receiving the end of your faith, even the salvation of your souls."

1 Peter 1:6-9 (KJV)

You may be the last picked for the job, the spouse, the children, and for the things you think you need, but Beloved, you shall be first to witness My glory, so hold on! Gain and maintain right perspective. Let your confession be:

"I may have been picked last, but the last shall be first, and the first shall be last!"

Proper perspective will spiritually prosper you. And Beloved, My delay is not a denial. Though it tarry, wait on it - it will surely not delay. I who have promised it, am faithful.

I love you, My *last pick*!

Love, Abba Father

Respond

What is the in-between of this letter? (Focus)

_____
_____
_____
_____
_____
_____

What is God saying about Himself? (Perspective)

_____
_____
_____
_____
_____
_____

What is God saying about me? (Perspective)

_____
_____
_____
_____
_____
_____

What advice is God giving me to live victoriously in this in-between? (Action)

_____
_____
_____
_____
_____
_____

From: God
To: The One Who Feels Forgotten

Hello My Beloved,

I am sending you a reminder in this day, at this moment, that I have not forgotten about you.

I know you see people around you getting blessed and thriving. I know you feel like I have turned a deaf ear to the things you have asked of Me. However, I assure you that I have heard you, and I am responding to you.

Take courage and have hope in Me. I am the same God who saw you through every trial and situation you have gone through. I am the God who has given you countless examples in My Word of my ability to remember and how I respond. Look at Sarah:

"And when Abram was ninety years old and nine, the Lord appeared to Abram, and said unto him, I am the Almighty God; walk before me, and be thou perfect.
² And I will make my covenant between me and thee, and will multiply thee exceedingly.
And God said unto Abraham, As for Sarai thy wife, thou shalt not call her name Sarai, but Sarah shall her name be.
¹⁶ And I will bless her, and give thee a son also of her: yea, I will bless her, and she shall be a mother of nations; kings of people shall be of her.
¹⁷ Then Abraham fell upon his face, and laughed, and said in his heart, Shall a child be born unto him that is an hundred years old? And shall Sarah, that is ninety years old, bear?
²¹ But my covenant will I establish with Isaac, which Sarah shall bear unto thee at this set time in the next year.
And the Lord visited Sarah as he had said, and the Lord did unto Sarah as he had spoken.
² For Sarah conceived, and bare Abraham a son in his old age, at the set time of which God had spoken to him.
³ And Abraham called the name of his son that was born unto him, whom Sarah bare to him, Isaac."
Genesis 17:1-2, 15-17, 21, 21:1-3 (KJV)

The wait is for a reason. I am drawing something out of you to make room to deposit something greater. What do you think of your response to My *wait* in this season? Respond in joy, faithfulness, worship, and drawing near to Me. I love you. And like Sarah, you will deliver, but not apart from Me. I know what's best for you. Do you believe that? If so, live in the truth that you are remembered, and your maturation as My child is My highest priority. Believe that if you stick this out with Me and not faint, you will reap a harvest you didn't even plant. Trust Me. I see you.

"Fret not thyself because of evildoers, neither be thou envious against the workers of iniquity. For they shall soon be cut down like the grass, and wither as the green herb. Trust in the Lord, and do good; so shalt thou dwell in the land, and verily thou shalt be fed."
Psalm 37:1-3 (KJV)

"Behold, the LORD'S hand is not shortened, that it cannot save; neither his ear heavy, that it cannot hear."
Isaiah 59:1 (KJV)

"Then said he unto me, Fear not, Daniel: for from the first day that thou didst set thine heart to understand, and to chasten thyself before thy God, thy words were heard, and I am come for thy words."
Daniel 10:12 (KJV)

"Let us hold fast the profession of *our* faith without wavering; (for he *is* faithful that promised)."
Hebrews 10:23 (KJV)

Love, Abba Father

Respond

What is the in-between of this letter? (Focus)

_____

_____

_____

_____

_____

_____

What is God saying about Himself? (Perspective)

_____

_____

_____

_____

_____

_____

What is God saying about me? (Perspective)

_____

_____

_____

_____

_____

_____

What advice is God giving me to live victoriously in this in-between?
(Action)

_____

_____

_____

_____

_____

_____

From: God
To: My Adorned Bride

My Bride,

I love you with an everlasting love, and I am gifting you with My Spirit for the asking. You - My Bride, are the most highly paid-for prize I possess. I gave My only begotten Son for your heart. I wanted nothing - no sin, no weight, no barrier, to stand in the way of fellowship with you. My Bride, you are learning of Me and I could not be more delighted. Now, continue in Me.

You have learned My Heart, and that I made an inerrant order regarding how things are to live out: God, man, woman, children. But things were reversed in the garden when the woman spoke to the serpent, ate the forbidden fruit and gave to her husband to eat, and they fell. I have filled the catastrophic gap between us with the blood of My Son Jesus. But now My Bride, My heart is breaking again because the woman is speaking to the serpent again. There is a rise of the woman that I do not stand behind because she is stepping where she cannot be protected where My grace does not apply. You My Bride, are learning My heart, that I desire alignment, and you have a choice before you: This world, or Me? (James 4:7 KJV)

Once learning My heart, you learn what type of heart you have. Is your heart stony? When seeds of My truth falls on it, do they rot quickly, but not deep enough to avoid being scorched by the sun? Is your heart wayside? When My truth falls on it, does it even penetrate, and birds eat it up? Is your heart thorny? When My truth falls on it, does it grow for a while with joy, then allow life's cares to choke it out? Or is your heart good, fertile ground? When My truth falls on it, does it grow downward and take in the nutrients I provide in the secret place, then stretch up, growing strong, towards My light and bear fruit in its time? (Luke 8:4-15(KJV)

My Bride, I am putting all I am on the table so you may know Me as fully as humanly possible. I reveal seven facets of My character to you in the Gospel of John; it's up to you to decide if you can submit to Me with understanding and truth. I am:

The Bread of Life (John 6:35 KJV)
The Light of the World (John 8:12; 9:5 KJV)
The Door (John 10:7, 9 KJV)
The Good Shepherd (John 10:11 KJV)
The Resurrection and The Life (John 11:25 KJV)
The Way, The Truth, & The Life (John 14:6 KJV)
The True Vine (John 15:1 KJV)

Court Me on the truths of who I say I am. Spend time with Me. Ask Me Questions, I will answer you. (Galatians 5:16 KJV)

I have a question for you, Beloved. *Will you abide?* Will you remain, stay, swallow, consent, receive, wait…will you abide? Will you burn the bridge to every other option now that you've learned of Me? Do you treasure this relationship, even if it costs you everything?

"Yes," is the most blessed response that a life yielded to Me can bring. "Yes," encompasses trust, faith, action, obedience, and love. If you submit, I will make My *I am*, your *You are.* All I want is, "Yes." Are you saying yes to be adorned in this dress?

Build the memorial stone of this truth! Prize it with your life! Words are beautiful, but I want you to live the vow of obedience concerning what you believe about Me! To love is to obey! DO you love Me?

Carry this truth with you! Seal it in your heart! I am yours, and you are Mine! ABIDE, My Bride! ABIDE! (John 15:4 KJV)

Love, Your Bridegroom

Respond

What is the in-between of this letter? (Focus)

_____
_____
_____
_____
_____
_____

What is God saying about Himself? (Perspective)

_____
_____
_____
_____
_____
_____

What is God saying about me? (Perspective)

_____
_____
_____
_____
_____
_____

What advice is God giving me to live victoriously in this in-between? (Action)

_____
_____
_____
_____
_____
_____

From: God
To: The one Who Is Ready for Their Life to Change

My Beloved,

Thank you for taking Me at My Word. The first step was telling the truth about where you are: You need Me. You believed enough to come, and that is a good first step.

> *"If we confess our sins, he is faithful and just to forgive us our sins, and to cleanse us from all unrighteousness."*
> *1 John 1:9* (KJV)

> *"Then I acknowledged my sin to You and did not hide my iniquity. I said, 'I will confess my transgressions to the LORD,' and You forgave the guilt of my sin. Selah."*
> *Psalm 32:5 (NIV)*

> *"He that covereth his sins shall not prosper: but whoso confesseth and forsaketh them shall have mercy."*
> *Proverbs 28:13 (KJV)*

> *"Draw nigh to God, and he will draw nigh to you. Cleanse your hands, ye sinners; and purify your hearts, ye double minded."*
> *James 4:8 (KJV)*

> *"And Jesus said unto them, I am the bread of life: he that cometh to me shall never hunger; and he that believeth on me shall never thirst."*
> *John 6:35 (KJV)*

You see My Beloved, when you recognize your need for Me, confess it, turn your back on it, and give Me your hand and control, I cleanse you.

Unfortunately, this world has conditioned you to doubt and only come to Me when there is a problem. If you are ready for your life to change, THAT is what we are busting up.

You are to *welcome and expect*. When I visited the house of Mary and Martha, they welcomed Me in. The difference; however, was that Mary assumed a posture of expectation, sitting at My feet and listening to what I had to say as Martha continued to work. When Martha spoke of her need for her sister to help her, I told her "No." Her sister had chosen the better thing, and I was not going to take it from her. The world can wait, Beloved. Time with Me is always worth the sacrifice. Welcoming Me is good; expecting Me to speak is better. Posturing yourself to listen to Me when I come is best. Have the expectation that if you ask Me to come, I will.

Graduate from duty to delight. Yes, until your will breaks and you come to Me because you want to, not because you have to. Force-feed yourself My Word, day and night. Get extra with it, even doing it at mealtime. I am so confident in the power of My Word that I know if you come into it with a heart ready to change, you will break open, fall in love with Me, and your faithful coming from duty will soon become your delight! When you stack the peace of My presence against the *peace* this world claims to give, you will fully forsake the world and live changed in My Light. In My Light, you will see Light.

Lastly Beloved, talk to Me out loud. Yes, I know your every thought even before you think it, but I want to hear your voice. With sound, the Heavens and the earth were created. Speak to Me, Beloved. I want to hear what you have to say. And My response will be found in My Word.

I love you, and I want you to love Me, too. I've removed the barrier of sin that kept you from Me. And if you accept My gift, we can live in communion together, forever. Say yes to your life changing and hold the note of your song of freedom. Selah.

Love, Abba Father

Respond

What is the in-between of this letter? (Focus)

_____

_____

_____

_____

_____

_____

What is God saying about Himself? (Perspective)

_____

_____

_____

_____

_____

_____

What is God saying about me? (Perspective)

_____

_____

_____

_____

_____

_____

What advice is God giving me to live victoriously in this in-between? (Action)

_____

_____

_____

_____

_____

_____

From: God
To: The One Who Won't Pour Out

My Beloved,

Freely you have received the living water of My love, so freely you must give. I have filled you to the brim of your capacity, yet you still want more to overflowing. But I want you to pour out, so I may pour in.

There are people who are thirsty in the dry place that I have led you. They are sitting, weary, thirsty, and stagnant with their cups facing up, desperate for a drink. You, my Beloved, are the pitcher, and I am the Living Water. Pour.

I am not sure how you developed this notion that if you give away all you have, you will be left with nothing. I am a never-ending supply for you to drink from. You will never be left with nothing. I will cause the rain of My love and truth to fill you, if you constantly pour.

I make ways in the wilderness, and rivers in the desert. I send forth My blessed into the dry places; they make them an oasis by leaving springs wherever they go. Are you making springs in the valley? I am sending rain in autumn to create pools.

Pour out, Beloved. I give more to those who give away what I give them. To they whose hearts are set on the pilgrimage, My mission: Pour out.

If you want overflow, I need to know that you will not keep it for yourself. I want to give you fresh water, so pour out all you have to the people, then come back to Me to be refilled. I refresh those who refresh others. Refresh others!

For My Word says:

> *Blessed are those who dwell in your house;*
> *they are ever praising you.*[a]

[5] Blessed are those whose strength is in you,
whose hearts are set on pilgrimage.
[6] As they pass through the Valley of Baka,
they make it a place of springs;
the autumn rains also cover it with pools.[b]
[7] They go from strength to strength,
till each appears before God in Zion.
Psalm 84:5-7(NIV)

"A generous person will prosper; whoever refreshes others will be refreshed."
Proverbs 11:25 (NIV)

"He that giveth unto the poor shall not lack: but he that hideth his eyes
shall have many a curse."
Proverbs 28:27 (KJV)

"Heal the sick, raise the dead, cleanse those who have leprosy, drive out
demons. Freely you have received; freely give."
Matthew 8:10 (NIV)

"Come, all of you who thirst, come to the waters; and you without money,
come, buy, and eat! Come, buy wine and milk, without money and without
cost!"
Isaiah 55:1 (NIV)

I have led you to the high place to be filled by Me, and experience your thirst being quenched and fully satisfied. Now, I am setting your heart on pilgrimage to dry places to give freely and liberally My Living Water. Pour out Beloved, and I will refresh your supply. Pour out.

Love, Abba Father

Respond

What is the in-between of this letter? (Focus)

_____

_____

_____

_____

_____

What is God saying about Himself? (Perspective)

_____

_____

_____

_____

_____

What is God saying about me? (Perspective)

_____

_____

_____

_____

_____

What advice is God giving me to live victoriously in this in-between? (Action)

_____

_____

_____

_____

_____

From: God
To: My Child Whom I Love and I Know Who Needs Me

Hello My Beloved,

I love you. I really, really love you. You did not do anything to earn this love; I freely give it to you. I see you. I really, really see you. I see your need and I have a gift for you: Strength.

Confess My Word over your life, Beloved. Confess My truths over your life. The power of death and life is in your tongue. Choose the life My Word gives and eat of its fruit.

Proclaim My Word that says:

"When you pass through the waters,
I will be with you;
and when you pass through the rivers,
they will not sweep over you.
When you walk through the fire,
you will not be burned;
the flames will not set you ablaze."
Isaiah 43:2 (NIV)

"Therefore everyone who hears these words of mine and puts them into practice is like a wise man who built his house on the rock. [25] *The rain came down, the streams rose, and the winds blew and beat against that house; yet it did not fall, because it had its foundation on the rock."*
Matthew 7:24-25 (NIV)

"Yet this I call to mind
and therefore I have hope:
[22] *Because of the Lord's great love we are not consumed,*
for his compassions never fail.
[23] *They are new every morning;*
great is your faithfulness.
[24] *I say to myself, 'The Lord is my portion;*
therefore I will wait for him.'
[25] *The Lord is good to those whose hope is in him,*
to the one who seeks him."

Lamentations 3:21-25 (NIV)

"But we have this treasure in jars of clay to show that this all-surpassing power is from God and not from us. ⁸ We are hard pressed on every side, but not crushed; perplexed, but not in despair; ⁹ persecuted, but not abandoned; struck down, but not destroyed."
2 Corinthians 4:7-9 (NIV)

Beloved, this Word WORKS! This Word is for YOU! I LOVE YOU! I will see you through the storms and uncertainties. I will be your strength! This is an opportunity to see Me perform a miracle, and for YOU to KNOW that I AM GOD!

Trust in Me, Beloved! Do not waver in your faith! You know who I am; I know who you are! We have history! You've seen Me save, rescue, HEAL and set free from afflictions! You KNOW My character. WE HAVE HISTORY.

"But blessed is the one who trusts in the LORD, whose confidence is in him."
Jeremiah 17:7 (NIV)

Love, Abba Father

Respond

What is the in-between of this letter? (Focus)

_____
_____
_____
_____
_____
_____

What is God saying about Himself? (Perspective)

_____
_____
_____

_____
_____
_____

What is God saying about me? (Perspective)

_____
_____
_____
_____
_____
_____

What advice is God giving me to live victoriously in this in-between? (Action)

_____
_____
_____
_____
_____
_____

From: God
To: My Come Back Kid

My Beloved,

Come back! This is a plea, and a prophecy. Your soul longs for Me in a dry and weary land where there is no water. Come back to Me.

I have loved you with an everlasting love, and drawn you with unfailing kindness. Come to Me, you who are weary and heavy laden, and I will give you rest. I love you and have never stopped loving you. No matter where fear has led you and the blows of wind pushed you, I am willing to plant and re-root you in good soil, on level ground.

Come back to Me.

Because you are precious and honored in My sight and I love you, I have given people in exchange for you -nations exchanged for your life. Do you not think I will fight for you to the ends of the earth? Did you not think I would be a good Father and rescue you from the ones who tried to take you out of My hand? Did you not think I would carry your captors away? Did you not think I would pick up the pieces of your life, rewrite your story, and construct a mosaic? Did you not think I would confuse your enemy and take away everything you held dear because I wanted you for Myself? I AM a jealous God! I AM JEALOUS FOR YOU! I gave My only Son for YOU! YOU! YOU are the reason that made forsaking Him so hard, yet His love for you was so easy, He willingly gave up His life for yours. He was your promissory note and came through at the appointed time with the necessary payment for Me to have YOU forever. NOT ONE that I have given Him will be plucked out of His hand, so do not jump out of My hand.

Isn't My love enough to keep you? Is not My love enough to draw you? You know who you are. You know the gifts I have given you. You were always on My mind, and you still are today.

Come back.

I will leave the 99 for you. I will come into the place that is darkest in you and give you light again. True light. I will graft you into what you have tried to get out of. Let Me be the strongest voice in your ear. Let go of every influence, thing, person, and problem that is trying to separate you from Me. Allow Me to mend your heart. I can handle it. I can handle your tears. I can handle your fears. I can handle your frustrations. I know this is hard for you to hear, but please, let me be your Father.

I have not forgotten you. I am not so upset that I would stay far from you. I want you now, and always have. Abide, make home, make full residence, buy the house in My love. No more renting, moving, or house guests. Just Me. Just you.

My Son - whom I love, left Me to come down to you. He then left his mother, to be wed to you. He situated Himself as head of the body, so your heart can function. With a functioning heart, you can now sense your body telling you there is pain here and there. Without My Son as head of your life, you cannot even sense the pain or danger you are in. Let HIM be the head of your life. Be His Church. Be His wife. He gave himself for you. He mastered leave and cleave, all for you. He is a willing husband to wash, clothe, and present you as a radiant Bride for Himself. He wants to make you holy and blameless. And still, He wants to fill you with His love, His Gift, His Spirit, so you may bring forth much fruit, and mother the promise that has been inside of you since before the beginning of time.

Come back. By plea. By prophecy.

Love, Abba Father

Respond

What is the in-between of this letter? (Focus)

_____

_____

_____

_____

_____

_____

What is God saying about Himself? (Perspective)

_____

_____

_____

_____

_____

_____

What is God saying about me? (Perspective)

_____

_____

_____

_____

_____

_____

What advice is God giving me to live victoriously in this in-between? (Action)

_____

_____

_____

_____

_____

_____

From: God
To: The Bitter

Hello My Beloved,

You feel unseen, unacknowledged, underappreciated, and unloved. I know. I see you. I instruct you in My Word to:

"Casting all your care upon him; for he careth for you."
1 Peter 5:7 (KJV)

"Dearly beloved, avenge not yourselves, but *rather* give place unto wrath: for it is written, Vengeance *is* mine; I will repay, saith the Lord."
Romans 12:19 (KJV)

But Beloved, you continue taking matters in your own hands, and seek to kill in your heart. If you are really honest, you want the person who is bombarding your heart and filling you with rage to feel how you feel, and teach them a lesson. This is not the way. This is not trusting me. My Word says,

"Let all bitterness and wrath and anger and clamor and slander be put away from you, along with all malice. Be kind to one another, tenderhearted, forgiving one another, as God in Christ forgave you."
Ephesians 4:31-32 (KJV)

The anecdote to bitterness is forgiveness and repentance. You have to trust that I am God, and I will work it out. I am not saying these things to condemn you, but to save you. I am a merciful God who is full of justice.

Let it go! Cast your cares on ME, because I care for YOU. Beloved, I have instructions in My Word regarding bitterness. What I need you to do is:
1. Read them with a heart to receive them as truth.
2. Believe and meditate on them. Review the scriptures over and over in your mind.
3. Heed them - do as I say. It will save your life.

My thoughts on bitterness:

Hebrews 12:14-15 ESV
"Strive for peace with everyone, and for the holiness without which no one will see the Lord. See to it that no one fails to obtain the grace of God; that no "root of bitterness" springs up and causes trouble, and by it many become defiled."

Ephesians 4:26 ESV
"Be angry and do not sin; do not let the sun go down on your anger."

Matthew 6:14-15 ESV
"For if you forgive others their trespasses, your heavenly Father will also forgive you, but if you do not forgive others their trespasses, neither will your Father forgive your trespasses."

Proverbs 10:12 ESV
"Hatred stirs up strife, but love covers all offenses."

Colossians 3:8 ESV
"But now you must put them all away: anger, wrath, malice, slander, and obscene talk from your mouth."

James 1:19-20 ESV
"Know this, my beloved brothers: let every person be quick to hear, slow to speak, slow to anger; for the anger of man does not produce the righteousness of God."

Colossians 3:13 ESV
"Bearing with one another and, if one has a complaint against another, forgiving each other; as the Lord has forgiven you, so you also must forgive."

James 4:7 ESV
"Submit yourselves therefore to God. Resist the devil, and he will flee from you."

Love, Abba Father

Respond

What is the in-between of this letter? (Focus)

_____
_____
_____
_____
_____
_____

What is God saying about Himself? (Perspective)

_____
_____
_____
_____
_____
_____

What is God saying about me? (Perspective)

_____
_____
_____
_____
_____
_____

What advice is God giving me to live victoriously in this in-between? (Action)

_____
_____
_____
_____
_____

From: God
To: The Gifted One

Hello My Beloved,

I want to talk to you briefly about G.I.F.T.s. I am the *Gift Giver.* I want you to know that I have given you many good gifts. What is a G.I.F.T.? It is a strategy to keep your heart and mind stayed on Me, and to keep you obedient to My Word when I say:

"Pray without ceasing. In everything give thanks: for this is the will of God in Christ Jesus concerning you. Quench not the Spirit. Despise not prophesyings. Prove all things; hold fast that which is good."
1 Thessalonians 5:17-21 (KJV)

Gratitude
"In everything give thanks: for this is the will of God in Christ Jesus concerning you."
1 Thessalonians 5:18 (KJV)

"And it came to pass, as he went to Jerusalem, that he passed through the midst of Samaria and Galilee. And as he entered into a certain village, there met him ten men that were lepers, which stood afar off: And they lifted up their voices, and said, Jesus, Master, have mercy on us. And when he saw them, he said unto them, Go shew yourselves unto the priests. And it came to pass, that, as they went, they were cleansed. And one of them, when he saw that he was healed, turned back, and with a loud voice glorified God, And fell down on his face at his feet, giving him thanks: and he was a Samaritan. And Jesus answering said, Were there not ten cleansed? but where are the nine? There are not found that returned to give glory to God, save this stranger. And he said unto him, Arise, go thy way: thy faith hath made thee whole."
Luke 17:11-19 (KJV)

Intimacy
"Ye have not chosen me, but I have chosen you, and ordained you, that ye should go and bring forth fruit, and *that* your fruit should remain: that whatsoever ye shall ask of the Father in my name, he may give it you."

John 15:16 (KJV)

"Draw nigh to God, and he will draw nigh to you.
Cleanse *your* hands, *ye* sinners; and purify *your* hearts, *ye* double
minded."
James 4:8 (KJV)

"Henceforth I call you not servants; for the servant knoweth
not what his lord doeth: but I have called you friends; for all things
that I have heard of my Father I have made known unto you."
John 15:15 (KJV)

"The LORD hath appeared of old unto me, *saying,* Yea, I have
loved thee with an everlasting love: therefore with lovingkindness
have I drawn thee."
Jeremiah 31:3 (KJV)

Focus
"For where your treasure is, there will your heart be also."
Matthew 6:21 (KJV)

"Set your affection on things above, not on things on the
earth."
Colossians 3:2 (KJV)

"The light of the body is the eye: if therefore thine eye be single,
thy whole body shall be full of light.
23 But if thine eye be evil, thy whole body shall be full of
darkness. If therefore the light that is in thee be darkness, how
great is that darkness!"
Matthew 6:22-23 (KJV)

Time
"Walk in wisdom toward them that are without, redeeming the
time."
Colossians 4:5 (KJV)

"See then that ye walk circumspectly, not as fools, but as wise,
redeeming the time, because the days are evil."
Ephesians 5:15-16 (KJV)

"And that, knowing the time, that now it is high time to awake out of sleep: for now is our salvation nearer than when we believed."
Romans 13:11 (KJV)

Take heed. Use your G.I.F.T.s. Obey My Word.

Love, Abba Father

Respond

What is the in-between of this letter? (Focus)

_____

_____

_____

_____

_____

_____

What is God saying about Himself? (Perspective)

_____

_____

_____

_____

_____

_____

What is God saying about me? (Perspective)

_____

_____

_____

_____

_____

_____

What advice is God giving me to live victoriously in this in-between? (Action)

_____

_____

_____

_____

_____

_____

From: God
To: The One Who Doesn't Know How to Be Still

Hello My Beloved,

Be still and know that I am God. You My beloved, lack confidence in My ability to be fully in control of every aspect of your life. Do you not know that I've known you since before you were in your mother's womb, and put purpose on your life?

Searching for your identity has caused you to be a busybody. You fear stealing away to hear Me. I see how being still keeps you awake at night and torments you. You have not rested in so long, beyond sleep. Your mind, heart, and soul have not rested. You have been in a constant state of stress. I have a remedy for that, Beloved:

> *"Come unto me, all ye that labour and are heavy laden, and I will give you rest.*
> *29 Take my yoke upon you, and learn of me; for I am meek and lowly in heart: and ye shall find rest unto your souls.*
> *30 For my yoke is easy, and my burden is light."*
> Matthew 11:28-30 (KJV)

MY yoke is easy, and MY burden is light, Beloved. They will not weigh you down, or keep you immobile and inactive. Don't you want the freedom and joy of purpose in Me? It starts with being still, so I can refresh you.

You serve and serve, and serve. I do take joy in your selflessness and love of service; however, you have to balance it out with intimacy with Me. Intimacy with Me is My highest priority for your life. In My Word, I say that:

> "The liberal soul shall be made fat: and he that watereth shall be watered also himself."
> Proverbs 11:25 (KJV)

> "For I have satiated the weary soul, and I have replenished every sorrowful soul."
> Jeremiah 31:25 (KJV)

Beloved, as you refresh, I will refresh you! But that all starts with being still and knowing that I am God. I am in control.

During prayer, one of My beloved asked me, "God, if I let go of my worries, fears, and control, what will be left of me?" I simply replied, "Me." I am at the end of your rope, Beloved. I am keeping you from falling into the pit despair, busyness and worry creates.

Will you still your mind, heart, and soul in Me today? Will you agree with My Spirit, and receive the sound mind I have available for you?

"For God hath not given us the spirit of fear; but of power, and of love, and of a sound mind."
2 Timothy 1:7 (KJV)

Beloved, will you let Me be in control? You are truly in good hands. You are the apple of My eye, and I see your every move. I want rest for you. I want assurance of My love to flood your heart. Let Me love you. Be Still.

"Be still, and know that I *am* God: I will be exalted among the heathen, I will be exalted in the earth."
Psalm 46:10 (KJV)

Love, Abba Father

Respond

What is the in-between of this letter? (Focus)

_____

_____

_____

_____

_____

_____

What is God saying about Himself? (Perspective)

_____

_____

_____

_____

_____

What is God saying about Me? (Perspective)

_____

_____

_____

_____

_____

What advice is God giving me to live victoriously in this in-between? (Action)

_____

_____

_____

_____

_____

From: God
To: The One Who is Satisfied with Bearing the Armor Instead of Wearing the Armor

Hello My Beloved,

I love you, and I get excited when you avail yourself and come to Me as a student to hear and receive My Word. However, there is one thing I have against you - you have grown far too comfortable with bearing My armor, instead of wearing My armor.

There is a point in every student's discipleship where they must be tested to show the teacher they understand, can rightly divide, and apply the information they have received. It is the difference between being a hearer or doer; bearing the armor, or wearing the armor.

> "But be ye doers of the word, and not hearers only, deceiving
> your own selves."
> James 1:22 (KJV)

You, My beloved, will be fought tooth and nail on the very things I am giving you. The information you receive will be challenged to show Me if the revelation is received and applied. This brawl for your soul and allegiance will come by none other than your enemy and Mine, Satan. You know I am victorious and I will fight for you, but there are some battles I will allow to see if you will suit up and stand, or sit down and succumb.

[10] Finally, my brethren, be strong in the Lord, and in the power of his might.

[11] Put on the whole armour of God, that ye may be able to stand against the wiles of the devil.

[12] For we wrestle not against flesh and blood, but against principalities, against powers, against the rulers of the darkness of this world, against spiritual wickedness in high places.

[13] Wherefore take unto you the whole armour of God, that ye may be able to withstand in the evil day, and having done all, to stand.

[14] Stand therefore, having your loins girt about with truth, and

having on the breastplate of righteousness;

15 And your feet shod with the preparation of the gospel of peace;

16 Above all, taking the shield of faith, wherewith ye shall be able to quench all the fiery darts of the wicked.

17 And take the helmet of salvation, and the sword of the Spirit, which is the word of God:

18 Praying always with all prayer and supplication in the Spirit, and watching thereunto with all perseverance and supplication for all saints.

Ephesians 6:10-18 (KJV)

You see My Beloved, it is not enough just to HAVE my Word, you must USE My Word to be successful against the many tactics of our enemy, the devil.

"Wherefore gird up the loins of your mind, be sober, and hope to the end for the grace that is to be brought unto you at the revelation of Jesus Christ."

1 Peter 1:13 (KJV)

Stop being satisfied with bearing, and start wearing My Word, Beloved. The armor works, fits, and is tried and true. And guess what? It is a gift from Me to you. I love you…now take what you've learned of Me, and be a doer.

Love, Abba Father

Respond

What is the in-between of this letter? (Focus)

_____

_____

_____

_____

_____

_____

What is God saying about Himself? (Perspective)

_____

_____

_____

_____

_____

_____

What is God saying about me? (Perspective)

_____

_____

_____

_____

_____

_____

What advice is God giving me to live victoriously in this in-between? (Action)

_____

_____

_____

_____

_____

_____

From: God
To: The One Who Will Not Try… Again

Hello My Beloved,

I love You deeply, and have loved you since before you were formed in your mother's womb. I have fearfully and wonderfully made and woven you together in the inward parts. The same creativity I used to make you, in my image and likeness, I deposited in you.

Just as I have spoken and formed things, because you are made in My image and likeness and have received me into your heart as Lord and Savior, you too can speak things and they form. This is a gift of walking with Me.

You, My beloved, have a dream that I put in you. It keeps you up at night and follows you all day. You doubted if it was from Me, but I have confirmed for you that it is from Me. I gave it to you because I love you, and I want you to use it to show My glory throughout the earth, starting with the ones in your direct sphere of influence. However, I have one ought against you, My Beloved: You will not try… again.

I know it seems like you've tried and tried, and the dream has not taken off. Others have not recognized it, but I used each seeming failure to teach you something, and draw you closer to Me. As I groom and grow you into maturity of the dream and gift I gave you, did you catch the lesson, or did you throw in the towel?

You are expecting this dream to fall out of the sky and make an enormous crash into your life, but it doesn't happen that way. You must put your hand to the plough for your future and never turn back. Don't remove your hands, even when it seems like it is not going according to your plan. And if you haven't tried at all, how do you expect to see, share, and return My glory?

So here is what I want you to do: Dream again with me. I want you to write it, then live it. Though it tarry, wait on it. It will not delay.

Try again with a faithful, diligent, non-complaining, non-quitting, pure heart, and watch Me blow your mind with My goodness. I who promised, am faithful. Spend time with Me, obey My Word, and watch your dreams become reality. Depend on ME for your strength and courage. Then try…again.

"And the LORD answered me, and said, Write the vision, and make *it* plain upon tables, that he may run that readeth it."
Habakkuk 2:2 (KJV)

"And Jesus said unto him, No man, having put his hand to the plough, and looking back, is fit for the kingdom of God."
Luke 9:62 (KJV)

"Go to the ant, thou sluggard; consider her ways, and be wise: Which having no guide, overseer, or ruler, provideth her meat in the summer, and gathereth her food in the harvest."
Proverbs 6:6-8 (KJV)

"Let us hold fast the profession of *our* faith without wavering; (for he *is* faithful that promised)."
Hebrews 10:23 (KJV)

"Being confident of this very thing, that he which hath begun a good work in you will perform it until the day of Jesus Christ."
Philippians 1:6 (KJV)

With Love, Abba Father

Respond

What is the in-between of this letter? (Focus)

_____

_____

_____

_____

_____

_____

What is God saying about Himself? (Perspective)

_____

_____

_____

_____

_____

_____

What is God saying about me? (Perspective)

_____

_____

_____

_____

_____

_____

What advice is God giving me to live victoriously in this in-between?
(Action)

_____

_____

_____

_____

_____

_____

From: God
To: The One with Poor Posture

Hello My Beloved,

You will never hear Me when you hold the perspective that I am hurting you. You have poor posture, and need to position your heart to hear Me.

You do not have a hearing problem, you hear many things. Too many things. The issue I'm addressing is your posture, and how you respond to My beckoning with defense and hypocrisy.

"This people draweth nigh unto me with their mouth, and honoureth me with *their* lips; but their heart is far from me."
Matthew 15:8 (KJV)

Beloved, this does not please Me. There are many wonderful things I want to tell you, but you cannot hear Me, because you look as if I am hurting you.

"Come now, and let us reason together, saith the Lord: though your sins be as scarlet, they shall be as white as snow; though they be red like crimson, they shall be as wool."
Isaiah 1:18 (KJV)

Let's talk this out. You believe that because I denied you some things, that I am incapable of a fruitful relationship with you. DO you know what I held back from you? DEATH. I held back DEATH. Death of your heart, your love for Me, your physical body. Beloved, just because I am holding back things you think you want and need, does not mean that I am not the SAME, GOOD, God who created and knows what is best for you and when it's best for you to receive it.

Changing your heart's posture will change your perception of Me. If you see Me as a bad God who never comes through for you, you will never hear Me when I say,

"Since thou wast precious in my sight, thou hast been

honourable, and I have loved thee: therefore will I give men for thee, and people for thy life."
Isaiah 43:4 (KJV)

If your heart is postured properly and perspective is correct of Me, you will hear Me when I say,

"Be strong and of a good courage, fear not, nor be afraid of them: for the LORD thy God, he *it is* that doth go with thee; he will not fail thee, nor forsake thee."
Deuteronomy 31:6 (KJV)

How then do you correct your posture? Go low. *Lower.* Posture your heart in humility and repentance. Seep your words in thanksgiving and truth. Learn Me and meditate on what I tell you as truth. Come away with Me, and silence all the distractions. You do not have a hearing problem, you have a posture problem. And Beloved, I am your Problem Solver.

"He that hath ears to hear, let him hear."
Matthew 11:15 (KJV)

Love, Abba Father

Respond

What is the in-between of this letter? (Focus)

_____
_____
_____
_____
_____
_____

What is God saying about Himself? (Perspective)

_____
_____
_____
_____
_____
_____

What is God saying about me? (Perspective)

_____
_____
_____
_____
_____
_____

What advice is God giving me to live victoriously in this in-between? (Action)

_____
_____
_____
_____
_____
_____

From: God
To: The One Who Needs to Know My Love for Them

Hello My Beloved,

I love you. I know you fight every day to believe I do, but believe Me - I love you.

I love you so much that I would become sin for you, and die the death that you deserved to atone My wrath and separation from you. Rise up from the grave My Love, to secure your eternal life with Me if you believe the love that I have for you.

First, you must believe that I AM, and that I am a rewarder of those who diligently seek Me. Believe that love I have for you and seek it.

If you seek Me with your whole heart, I will be found by you. I love you that much.

I love you so much, I send My Word to wash over you from the inside out. I send my Word as a servant to wash with blood and water your eye balls and lids so you can see, and your ears so you can hear. I wash your heart, joints, mouth, tongue, nose, and stomach. I am giving you an appetite for Me and My Love. Nothing else will satisfy you.

Draw near (James 4:8 KJV) and believe I am going through your mind and washing over your decision-making authority. Give Me the authority. My love can handle the authority and guide you in the way you should go. You will not error if you hear, love, and follow Me. Know My voice; this is My cry for intimacy with you. I know you are scared of intimacy, but it is the very thing that will free you and show you ME.

I love you so much that I would write My Word on your mind and heart, and remove the lies you have stored in your mind.

Let Me love you. The attention and recognition you've always longed for is found in Me. I see you, and I need you to love Me enough to let that be enough. Look back and remember all the things I saved, shielded and healed you from…how could you not know I love you?

It grieves Me that it is so hard for you to believe I love you. It is because I love you that I am patient with you, and I know you will give Me your whole heart and trust me, so I will not give up on you. I am longsuffering for you, because I love you. I love you. Let Me love you, please. Let Me love you.

Just take My Word for what it says and apply it to your heart like ointment. Let Me heal you.

I love you.

Abba, Father

Respond

What is the in-between of this letter? (Focus)

_____

_____

_____

_____

_____

_____

What is God saying about Himself? (Perspective)

_____

_____

_____

_____

_____

What is God saying about me? (Perspective)

_____

_____

_____

_____

_____

What advice is God giving me to live victoriously in this in-between?
(Action)

_____

_____

_____

_____

_____

From: God
To: The Not-Yet-Married

Hello My Beloved,

Oh, I need you to believe Me when I tell you through My prophet in Jeremiah 29:11 (KJV):

"For I know the thoughts that I think toward you, saith the LORD, thoughts of peace, and not of evil, to give you an expected end."

I am inviting you on a love adventure. Your singleness is an ideal advantage, because it affords you the opportunity to be undivided and undistracted from all I am inviting you to do.

Do not get upset and mad at My apostle Paul when he encourages you in 1 Corinthians 7 (KJV):

"7 For I would that all men were even as I myself. But every man hath his proper gift of God, one after this manner, and another after that. 8 I say therefore to the unmarried and widows, it is good for them if they abide even as I. 34 There is difference also between a wife and a virgin. The unmarried woman careth for the things of the Lord, that she may be holy both in body and in spirit: but she that is married careth for the things of the world, how she may please her husband. 35 And this I speak for your own profit; not that I may cast a snare upon you, but for that which is comely, and that ye may attend upon the Lord without distraction. 39 The wife is bound by the law as long as her husband liveth; but if her husband be dead, she is at liberty to be married to whom she will; only in the Lord. 40 But she is happier if she so abide, after my judgment: and I think also that I have the Spirit of God."

Beloved, develop a holy urgency to do all the things I have put on your heart to do! Serve selflessly, hug your loved ones more, serve those in your sphere of influence more, draw closer to Me in intimacy and joy, budget for blessing others, give of yourself and resources as I lead, with a cheerful heart. Do the radical thing! Give Me the radical, "YES!" Open your eyes to SEE the needs around you! You have the time! I will give you the energy! Burn-out is NOT your portion! Lack is NOT your portion! I have given you everything you NEED pertaining to life and godliness. You WILL succeed.

Beloved, just say yes to the most fulfilling love adventure you will enter in your life on Earth. Say yes to Me. I will clam your desires. My Holy Spirit - your comforter and teacher, will help you through seemingly low and dry places. I am your water - drink.

Will you come on this adventure with Me while you are not yet married? I promise if you lean into My love, you will not be disappointed.

Love, Abba Father

Respond

What is the in-between of this letter? (Focus)

_____
_____
_____
_____
_____
_____

What is God saying about Himself? (Perspective)

_____
_____
_____
_____
_____
_____

What is God saying about me? (Perspective)

_____
_____
_____
_____
_____
_____

What advice is God giving me to live victoriously in this in-between? (Action)

_____
_____
_____
_____
_____
_____

From: God
To: The One on the Fence

My Beloved,

Yes, you! It has been a long time since you have felt someone tell you they loved you and meant it. You carry suspicion in your heart, waiting on someone to fail you so you can be proven right and justify the walls you have built. I, The LORD your God, am here to tell you that you are wrong. I am here to love you, endlessly. But, you have the choice to love Me back.

I need you to get off the fence. In your devotion, decision making, habits, and your time. Get off the fence. I want you on my side, the side of light. I want you on My team, the team of righteousness. I have a plan for you, but you will never find it on the fence.

"And if it seem evil unto you to serve the LORD, choose you this day whom ye will serve; whether the gods which your fathers served that were on the other side of the flood, or the gods of the Amorites, in whose land ye dwell: but as for me and my house, we will serve the LORD."
Joshua 24:15 (KJV)

Beloved, choose today who you are going to serve. Are you going to serve Me, your Creator, Redeemer, Healer, Provider, or are you going to serve money? Will you serve yourself, or the habit feeding your emptiness?

There is not just another way, there is the ONLY way. There's no different or better, but the BEST way...and His name is Jesus Christ.

Beloved, as soon as you lay your life down the way you want to live is where I pick up the pieces, put back together what is useful, and make you into someone new whom you barely recognize. You have been waiting to be seen, well I see you. You have been waiting to be heard, well I hear you. You have been waiting to be remembered for the things you do to love and help people. Well Beloved, I will remember you. There is nothing you surrender that I cannot use and make better.

"And Elijah came unto all the people, and said, How long halt ye between two opinions? If the Lord be God, follow him: but if Baal, then follow him. And the people answered him not a word."
1 Kings 18:21 (KJV)

Answer a word, Beloved. Give Me your, "Yes." I can use what you lay down. Look, I know you've been on the fence that I am good. You know I am real. You know I am God. But I need you to be fully persuaded that I love you, because I do. You are waiting for something to happen, but you know what you need to do. Get off the fence on My side of the yard. Step into my territory.

16 Therefore, the promise comes by faith, so that it may be by grace and may be guaranteed to all Abraham's offspring—not only to those who are of the law but also to those who have the faith of Abraham. He is the father of us all. 17 As it is written: "I have made you a father of many nations."[a] He is our father in the sight of God, in whom he believed—the God who gives life to the dead and calls into being things that were not.
18 Against all hope, Abraham in hope believed and so became the father of many nations, just as it had been said to him, "So shall your offspring be."[b] 19 Without weakening in his faith, he faced the fact that his body was as good as dead—since he was about a hundred years old—and that Sarah's womb was also dead. 20 Yet he did not waver through unbelief regarding the promise of God, but was strengthened in his faith and gave glory to God, 21 being fully persuaded that God had power to do what he had promised. 22 This is why "it was credited to him as righteousness."
Romans 4:16-22 (NIV)

Choose, Beloved. I chose you, choose Me back. I love you endlessly. The sooner you give Me your whole heart, the sooner My love will unlock the beautiful plans I have for you. And at My goodness, you will wonder why you did not choose this beautiful life sooner. I'm here. Are you ready?

Love, Abba, Your Father

Respond

What is the in-between of this letter? (Focus)

_____

_____

_____

_____

_____

_____

What is God saying about Himself? (Perspective)

_____

_____

_____

_____

_____

_____

What is God saying about me? (Perspective)

_____

_____

_____

_____

_____

_____

What advice is God giving me to live victoriously in this in-between? (Action)

_____

_____

_____

_____

_____

_____

PART 2

During my growth journey, I searched the Word of God for how He wanted me to live. When I tell you that there is so very much to learn and grow from, trust me - there is. One place I stumbled on in scripture while seeking the Lord's wisdom concerning how we live, is in the book of Revelation. Now if you are anything like me, you shuddered in fear at this particular book in the Bible because let's be honest - we want to know what happens at the end, but not every scary detail. Well God eased me into Revelation, which in retrospect wasn't all that scary after all. He caused me to rest in chapters two and three, His letters to the seven churches.

Can we just reflect for a moment how cool it is that back then, God specialized in letter writing through His servants, and still does today? Jesus used an exiled servant and disciple (John the Apostle) to pen His heart to the seven churches of Asia Minor. What I love about this is that when you read these letters, you cannot help but see yourself in one or more of them. In the letters, Jesus commends, corrects, and instructs the churches how to behave, concluding by telling the churches their reward for being faithful and obedient to His instructions.

My in-between stage that I still tend to drift in and out of (and you may have too, if you've read this far), is that I often need gentle, yet firm reminders of God's wisdom for my life and conduct. Our gracious God did just that as He wrote these letters to His beloved church over the tablet of my heart. Pull the wisdom for yourself and respond to what He is saying to you.

FOR THE SEVEN CHURCHES

From: God
To: The One Who Forgot Their First Love

Hello My Beloved,

There is something about remembrance that shows a person how much you love them. Like when you **remember** a unique detail about the other person that seems small to you, but significant them, like a birthday or favorite color, **responding** with an act of service or a gift. Everyone desires this kind of love, even Me, your God. My dear Beloved, you've been doing well in most things, and I see you; however, you have forgotten the main thing: Me. Like My beloved children, I have opened an opportunity for you to remember and respond. So take heed, because My love for you is deep, and I want you to see and enjoy Me.

"Unto the angel of the church of Ephesus write; These things saith he that holdeth the seven stars in his right hand, who walketh in the midst of the seven golden candlesticks;
2 I know thy works, and thy labour, and thy patience, and how thou canst not bear them which are evil: and thou hast tried them which say they are apostles, and are not, and hast found them liars:
3 And hast borne, and hast patience, and for my name's sake hast laboured, and hast not fainted.
4 Nevertheless I have somewhat against thee, because thou hast left thy first love.

⁵ Remember therefore from whence thou art fallen, and repent, and do the first works; or else I will come unto thee quickly, and will remove thy candlestick out of his place, except thou repent.
⁶ But this thou hast, that thou hatest the deeds of the Nicolaitanes, which I also hate.
⁷ He that hath an ear, let him hear what the Spirit saith unto the churches; To him that overcometh will I give to eat of the tree of life, which is in the midst of the paradise of God."
Revelation 2:1-7 (KJV)

Beloved, My Word for the forgetful has not changed, and remains when I tell you:

"Whoever has My commandments and keeps them is the one who loves Me. The one who loves Me will be loved by My Father, and I will love him and reveal Myself to him."
John 14:15 (KJV)

Do you see, Beloved? If your candlestick is removed due to a lack of repentance, turning from sin (knowing what you need to do and not doing it) and back towards Me, you will not see Me. I created you to know and love Me, which includes seeing Me. My Word says in Matthew 5:8 (KJV):

"Blessed are the pure in heart: for they shall see God."

So, when I tell you to return to the first works:
- Walk in Unity.
- Do not grieve the Holy Spirit.
- Put on the New Man.
- Walk in Love.
- Walk in Light.
- Walk in Wisdom.
- Put on the Whole Armor of God.

It is not to be done from a works-based mentality, but from a pure heart that has the motivation to love Me.

Your job is to:
1. Remember from where you've fallen.

2. Repent.
3. Do the first works.

I do not leave them as a mystery, Beloved. They are outlined in the book of Ephesians. Your obedience comes with the reward of not only seeing Me and My activity now and in the time to come, but will be afforded the opportunity to eat from the tree of life that is in the midst of My paradise.

Be encouraged, Beloved - I see that your work is not mild labor, but laborious taking a stand for Me. I see you shedding light on the liars who call themselves apostles. I see how you can't stand evil, as do I. You are like me in this, and I love it! I see that you hate the deeds of them who mix the profane with the holy and I love it, because I do too!

You can keep seeing and shining for Me if you turn back to Me - your first love, and do the first works.

Love, Abba Father

Respond

What is the in-between of this letter? (Focus)

_____

_____

_____

_____

_____

_____

What is God saying about Himself? (Perspective)

_____

_____

_____

_____

_____

_____

What is God saying about me? (Perspective)

_____

_____

_____

_____

_____

_____

What advice is God giving me to live victoriously in this in-between? (Action)

_____

_____

_____

_____

_____

_____

From: God
To: The One Who Has to Shine Differently

Hello My Beloved,

I love you so much. I see you, and I am pleased with you. I am the first and the last. I was dead, and I am alive. You will have more in common with Me than you think you will, but hang in there, because I need you to shine differently.

"But rejoice, inasmuch as ye are partakers of Christ's sufferings; that, when his glory shall be revealed, ye may be glad also with exceeding joy."
1 Peter 4:13 (KJV)

I know what you're doing, and I see what it costs you. You see your poverty; I see your wealth.

"Blessed are the poor in spirit: for theirs is the kingdom of heaven."
Matthew 5:3 (KJV)

"Blessed are those who are persecuted because of righteousness, for theirs is the kingdom of heaven."
Matthew 5:10 (KJV)

Beloved, I know it hurts when the ones who disguised themselves as brethren, the place of worship as a hospital, even a home, turn on you. They show themselves as who they really are: the Synagogue of Satan - ones with the form of godliness but that denied the power of the true living God. Their hearts are far from Me. Your shine is a bit different because you are familiar with your enemy, the ones who disguised themselves as family.

Beloved, I have no rebuke, just commendation, warning and commission. You will be persecuted by the ones once loyal to God, but are now loyal to the government. There are two things I need you to do:

1. Fear not.
2. Be faithful, but not the average kind of faithful. Faithful

even if it costs you everything…even your life.

A rush of fear will try to overtake you, but hold on and fear not, Beloved. I tell you because I love and want you to be fortified, ready and faithful. You will be:

- Cast into prison.
- Tried.
- Suffer tribulation for ten days.

Although it is scary Beloved, be faithful even unto death. Your shine will not go unseen in eternity as you wear the crown of life I have prepared for you. Your greatest reward is that you will not be hurt by the second death. While your punisher is forever being yielded into the lake of fire with his followers, you will not be touched. You will rest with Me.

"Remember the word that I said unto you, the servant is not greater than his lord. If they have persecuted me, they will also persecute you."
John 15:20a (KJV)

I love you so much, and I am pleased with the way you shine through persecution for My name's sake. You are wealthy with a different currency, My faithful one. I know it hurts now, but fear not and be faithful, because it will all be worth it in the end. Your sharing in My suffering results in sharing in My glory. Release the *why me*, and embrace the *why not me*. It is an honor to share in My suffering.

"If we suffer, we shall also reign with him: if we deny him, he also will deny us."
2 Timothy 2:12 (KJV)

~Fear not, Be faithful~

"For which cause we faint not; but though our outward man perish, yet the inward man is renewed day by day. For our light affliction, which is but for a moment, worketh for us a far more exceeding and eternal weight of glory."
2 Corinthians 4:16-17 (KJV)

Love, Abba Father

Respond

What is the in-between of this letter? (Focus)

_____
_____
_____
_____
_____
_____

What is God saying about Himself? (Perspective)

_____
_____
_____
_____
_____
_____

What is God saying about me? (Perspective)

_____
_____
_____
_____
_____
_____

What advice is God giving me to live victoriously in this in-between? (Action)

_____
_____
_____
_____
_____
_____

From: God
To: The One Whose Pulpit Has Too Many Microphones

Hello Beloved,

I see that you live where Satan's rule is active and saturates society. You are in his headquarters. I see that you hold up My name. I see that even amongst evil you have not denied My faith, even when you've seen others persecuted and put to death for it.

I see you Beloved, and I have some things against you. Even though you have held My truth and personally have not denied My faith, you have allowed some things I hate. You have allowed those who put stumbling blocks before My people to infiltrate the fold of believers. You have also allowed those who mix the profane with the holy to have a platform among you, thus deceiving My people. You have not stopped nor silenced them. You have too many microphones on your pulpit, and My sheep are being led astray. I am NOT pleased with this.

12 And to the angel of the church in Pergamos write; these things saith he which hath the sharp sword with two edges;

13 I know thy works, and where thou dwellest, even where Satan's seat is: and thou holdest fast my name, and hast not denied my faith, even in those days wherein Antipas was my faithful martyr, who was slain among you, where Satan dwelleth.

14 But I have a few things against thee, because thou hast there them that hold the doctrine of Balaam, who taught Balac to cast a stumbling block before the children of Israel, to eat things sacrificed unto idols, and to commit fornication.

15 So hast thou also them that hold the doctrine of the Nicolaitanes, which thing I hate.

16 Repent; or else I will come unto thee quickly, and will fight against them with the sword of my mouth.

17 He that hath an ear, let him hear what the Spirit saith unto the churches; to him that overcometh will I give to eat of the hidden manna, and will give him a white stone, and in the stone a new name written, which no man knoweth saving he that receiveth it.

Revelation 2:12-17 (KJV)

You come from a place where you have power to influence many people, but you are allowing the influence of others to influence you and cause people to be confused and fall away. Use your influence for My glory.

You must not be friends with this world, and must forsake intermingling truth and lies in My sanctuary. Divorce this world and remain married to ME.

"Ye adulterers and adulteresses, know ye not that the friendship of the world is enmity with God? Whosoever therefore will be a friend of the world is the enemy of God."
James 4:4 (KJV)

2 And be not conformed to this world: but be ye transformed by the renewing of your mind, that ye may prove what is that good, and acceptable, and perfect, will of God.
Romans 12:2 (KJV)

Remain faithful, My beloved. Faithfulness goes beyond preserving your confession. It's protecting the flock and contending for the faith. Do not waste the intelligence and the influence I have given you. You've been a powerhouse when dealing with your faithfulness, but bow out when it comes to dealing with the error among you. As did my servant Nehemiah, clear out the temple and route out all liars and false teachers. Those who hold the principles of darkness in setting stumbling blocks for My children, and mixing lies with My truth, causing some to fall.

Repent. Turn away from your sin of apathy, and turn to Me. Turn completely to Me, and do what I ask you to do.

If you do not, I will use the sharp, two-edged sword of My word to destroy the offender, you and them, because I will not stand My sheep being led astray. But if you obey me, not only will I give you all of My Son Jesus, the hidden manna, the one the will fully satisfy you, but I will give you access to My eternal kingdom, a white stone. In that access, a new name that only you and I will know, because I love you, and it is that personal to Me.

Remember, Beloved:

- Hold to My name.
- Do not deny My faith.
- SPEAK AGAINST AND SILENCE THE EVIL ONES AMONG THE CHURCH, SNATCH THEIR MIC AND SHUT THEM OUT!
- Repent.
- Enjoy the rewards of obedience to Me: My Son, access to My kingdom, and a new name given to you by Me in love.

Love, Abba Father

Respond

What is the in-between of this letter? (Focus)

_____

_____

_____

_____

_____

_____

What is God saying about Himself? (Perspective)

_____

_____

_____

_____

_____

_____

What is God saying about me? (Perspective)

_____

_____

_____

_____

_____

_____

What advice is God giving me to live victoriously in this in-between? (Action)

_____

_____

_____

_____

_____

_____

From: God
To: The One Whose Works I Know

Hello My Beloved,

I know thy charity, service, faith, patience, and thy works; the last to be more than the first.

You live in a place that was once insignificant, but grew into notoriety because of skill and influence. The error is, that skill and influence was gained without Me. Corruption has entered into the hearts of man; the work that should have been done unto Me is now being done unto the gods of the guilds.

People are making their work unto gods of lust, greed, pride, money, power, and more. These gods are enticing My church - My Bride is prostituting herself for a paycheck.

There is no room for you amongst these gods, but some of My children have allowed the voices of misaligned and uncovered influences to speak over My voice and pollute My platform. I am God over all, and I will severely punish any and all persons who seduce My children into making idols out of work.

I made you for My enjoyment, but all who follow the uncovered and misaligned into the teaching and seduction of the gods of the guilds will suffer the same punishment. My eyes are fiery with judgement for the disobedient, and My feet are as fine brass for you to see yourself! See yourself and work out your salvation with fear and trembling!

Repent! Completely turn from the immoral talk and actions that you participate in at work, and I will not punish you as I will the disobedient. The guilds may give you job security in this world, but I will give you God security in the next.

I know your works, charity, service, faith, patience, and that your latter works are more than your first works. I commend the work that was done unto Me. I see and reward it with My power that that I received from Almighty God, that will crush enemies and false gods, and I will give you the Morning Star - Myself. You will have Light and BE light in the midst of darkness. My light in you will extinguish darkness.

I will destroy the harlot-seductress that have led too many astray from leading you astray, but you must hold on to what you have left until I return. Don't turn over another brethren to the gods of the guilds and their lewd ways. Work the work of the One who has sent you while it is day, because the night comes where no man can work.

Rid yourself of corruption, My beloved. Do not give a platform to the devil to deceive you. I am God of ALL and I will give you work that pleases Me. Hold on to what you have until I return. Overcome, and receive My Power and My Light.

Revelation 2:18-29 (KJV)

Love, Abba Father

Respond

What is the in-between of this letter? (Focus)

_____

_____

_____

_____

_____

_____

What is God saying about Himself? (Perspective)

_____

_____

_____

_____

_____

_____

What is God saying about me? (Perspective)

_____

_____

_____

_____

_____

_____

What advice is God giving me to live victoriously in this in-between? (Action)

_____

_____

_____

_____

_____

_____

From: God
To: The Lazy Watchman

Hello My Beloved,

I am not pleased with your work. I love you, so I am coming to correct you. Your work does not please Me at all. You have a reputation that you are alive and well, but I see you and Beloved, you are sick and dead. Not dying, dead. You are as spiritually dry as a withered fig tree.

I come by you expecting fruit in this critical time, because you look alive, but you are dead. And if you are not careful, the little that is alive among you will die as well.

> *"And unto the angel of the church in Sardis write; these things saith he that hath the seven Spirits of God, and the seven stars; I know thy works, that thou hast a name that thou livest, and art dead.*
> *2 Be watchful, and strengthen the things which remain, that are ready to die: for I have not found thy works perfect before God.*
> *3 Remember therefore how thou hast received and heard, and hold fast, and repent. If therefore thou shalt not watch, I will come on thee as a thief, and thou shalt not know what hour I will come upon thee.*
> *4 Thou hast a few names even in Sardis which have not defiled their garments; and they shall walk with me in white: for they are worthy.*
> *5 He that overcometh, the same shall be clothed in white raiment; and I will not blot out his name out of the book of life, but I will confess his name before my Father, and before his angels.*
> *6 He that hath an ear, let him hear what the Spirit saith unto the churches."*
> Revelation 3:1-6 (KJV)

> *7 Ye hypocrites, well did Esaias prophesy of you, saying,*
> *8 This people draweth nigh unto me with their mouth, and honoureth me with their lips; but their heart is far from me.*
> *9 But in vain they do worship me, teaching for doctrines the commandments of men.*
> *10 And he called the multitude, and said unto them, Hear, and understand:*
> *11 Not that which goeth into the mouth defileth a man; but that which cometh out of the mouth, this defileth a man.*

Matthew 15:7-11 (KJV)

Beloved, there are a few things I am asking you to do to save yourself and what is left:
1. Be watchful.
2. Strengthen the things which remain, that are ready to die.
3. Remember what you have received and heard.
4. Hold fast to what you received and heard.
5. Repent.

That Beloved, is your recipe of getting past your worst enemy - yourself. You have not been led astray by doctrines of those who mix truth and lies or those who create stumbling blocks for My beloved. Your enemy is your heart! You are My money makers, skilled and trusted with separating pure from fillers to create a pure product, but you cannot separate sin from righteousness and God from money. You praise Me with your lips, but your hearts are far from Me. Your issue is not only rejecting Me by your lazy forgetfulness, but trying to replace Me with empty, dead money. You have not esteemed Me as your highest treasure.

But, there are a few among you that have not dirtied the garment of their heart that I see. Those people will walk with Me in white. If the rest of you repent, you will be clothed in white, and I will not blot your name out of the Book of Life. I will also confess your name before My Father, which is an honor far greater than your spirit could handle.

Beloved, I will separate the sheep from the goat as skillfully as you can separate gold from silver. Repent! Only sheep get in. Not all who cry out Lord, Lord will make it in.

Arise oh sleeping watchman, repent from your lazy slumber and warn! Check the hearts being led away among you by their unchecked lust. Hold onto the teaching and principles that give you life! Christ will give you light! Will you be My light?

Love, Abba Father

Respond

What is the in-between of this letter? (Focus)

_____

_____

_____

_____

_____

_____

What is God saying about Himself? (Perspective)

_____

_____

_____

_____

_____

_____

What is God saying about me? (Perspective)

_____

_____

_____

_____

_____

_____

What advice is God giving me to live victoriously in this in-between?
(Action)

_____

_____

_____

_____

_____

_____

From: God
To: The One at the Open Door

Hello My Beloved,

> You sought Me when no one was searching,
> You believed Me amidst unbelievers,
> You chose Me amidst idols,
> You affirm My character among doubters.

> Your confession is steadfast and consistent,
> Your steps are steadied,
> You love Me among liars,
> You told the truth among those that hate Me.

> You please Me amidst the unfaithful,
> And behold I set before you an open door that no man can shut.

You My Beloved, are used to doors being closed on you. You bring truth wherever you go and speak the native language of Heaven - truth. Those of the Synagogue of Satan have shut you down. These are the people who say they are of the faith, but are not. They have shut you out of the place of vision for the lost and weary and shut you down from speaking truth, but that changes today.

Though you are weak, the door I have opened for you is not for you to flee, but for you to be who you are in Me. Speak your native language of truth! The ones who shut you up and out before will come to you in honor and know that I have loved you. Yes, I love you because though you have been persecuted, you have not denied My name and obeyed Me. I will put you on display as My beloved.

As a reward for your obedience amidst persecution, I will protect you from the time of temptation that will come to the world to show Me who is of the world, and who is of Me. Your faithfulness has proven your side.

In addition to that pardon, I will make you a pillar in My house forever, and you will never have to worry about being shut out, and will live there forever. Not only has your faithfulness heaped on those expressions of My love, but I will also write on you the name of the city of God, the New Jerusalem, where you will be citizens. As an added bonus, you will have MY new name written on you.

All I need you to do is hold onto what you have, so no one will take your crown. I know you are weak, but hold on, Beloved. It is soon time to cash in on the faithfulness you displayed out of clean hands and a pure heart. You will never hunger or thirst again. Because you chose intimacy and obedience as your portion in the earth, no matter the side of persecution you did not order, you will enjoy the fruit of your choice now, and when I return for you.

Your obedience pleases Me. I love you deeply, My faithful example.

"But the God of all grace, who hath called us unto his eternal glory by Christ Jesus, after that ye have suffered a while, make you perfect, stablish, strengthen, settle you."
1 Peter 5:10 (KJV)

Revelation 3:7-13 (KJV)

Love, Abba Father

Respond

What is the in-between of this letter? (Focus)

_____

_____

_____

_____

_____

_____

What is God saying about Himself? (Perspective)

_____

_____

_____

_____

_____

_____

What is God saying about me? (Perspective)

_____

_____

_____

_____

_____

_____

What advice is God giving me to live victoriously in this in-between? (Action)

_____

_____

_____

_____

_____

_____

From: God
To: The Rich Man, Sick Man

Hello My Beloved,

You have access to the cool waters of refreshment, and the hot waters of healing. However, instead of choosing one or the other and going the distance with Me to reach refreshment and healing, lazily and prideful with your wealth, you draw from Me without drawing to Me. Instead of being refreshment and healing to the world, you are becoming sickness to them, throwing wealth and insufficient remedy around instead of administering Me (Refreshment and Healing). Your man-made efforts for what only I can give leaves you with a lukewarm product, not fit to consume. Even I will spit it out of My mouth. Your man-made efforts to obtain only what I can give, leaves you and others sick.

Your ways of seeing leave you blind. The impurity of your garments causes them to fray and leave you naked. Your eyes need healing, that's your perspective. Your garments need cleansing, that's your behaviors. Beloved, your wealth and resources are making you as sick as the deception of lukewarm water refreshing thirst.

Do you want to be rich? Gold tried by fire is a heart purified by Me, that I remove all impurities from. It is true wealth. Do you want right perspective? Stop washing yourself (that's the first step, Peter), and apply the balm of My Word. It is like a salve that when you obey it, will cause you to see everything clearly. You trying to wash your perspective with your worldly gain and knowledge, will leave you blind and far from Me. Do you want the shame of your nakedness to disappear? Clothe yourself in the white raiment of My righteousness, Beloved. Only I can cover your shame and need. Look at where your efforts got you... deceived!

I am correcting you because I love you and do not want to be separated from you. But I will separate from you if you continue to think and respond as though you can buy and outsource your way out of authentic intimacy and relationship with Me. I only correct those I love. Use your energies to be moved about your correction and repent!

I am knocking on the door of your heart. Yes, I came close to you. Yes, I came into your mess, self-sufficiency, self-dependence, and wrecked shop. Now if you open the door to Me, we will rest and eat together. I will show you how to eat (take in) and digest (process and apply) My Word to you. I will come in.

Overcome yourself, and I will allow you to sit with Me in My throne, just like I overcame Myself and sit at My Father's throne. You see, I too was rich. I humbled myself to become a man, was stripped, and saw the decrepit state of this dying world. I was tried by the ultimate fire and came out gold. I can relate to being high and in love being called low. My worth didn't diminish, it was glorified in God. You do not have to have it all together, and don't have to save face so others can see your wealth, competence and notoriety. Draw near to refreshing if you need it. Draw near to healing if you need it. You have access, but do you recognize your need, and will you depend on yourself or Me to get it? He who has an ear, let him hear what the Spirit is saying to the churches.

"He that hath an ear, let him hear what the Spirit saith unto the churches."

Revelation 2:7, 11, 17, 29, 3:6, 13, 22 (KJV)
Matthew 11:15, 13:9-16 (KJV)
Mark 4:9, 23 (KJV)

Love, Abba Father

Respond

What is the in-between of this letter? (Focus)

_____
_____
_____
_____
_____
_____

What is God saying about Himself? (Perspective)

_____
_____
_____
_____
_____
_____

What is God saying about me? (Perspective)

_____
_____
_____
_____
_____
_____

What advice is God giving me to live victoriously in this in-between? (Action)

_____
_____
_____
_____
_____
_____

PART 3
FOR THE MEN

God loves His sons; I love my brothers. While God has positioned strong men in the lives of growing men to disciple and lead them, sometimes He uses a sister to encourage a brother in the faith.

I do not have any biological brothers, but I do have several male cousins who I know God loves and pursues. Who is the man or men in your life that you know God desires to use in a powerful way or is currently using in a powerful way? Write their names below:

_____

_____

_____

_____

_____

_____

_____

_____

As a sister in Christ, it is our duty to pray for our brothers, fathers, uncles, sons, the males in our lives in general.

When God downloaded this next letter on my heart, I was deeply humbled and honored to be able to one day share it with the men in my life. Their salvation and obedience to God has the ability to not only shift the spiritual trajectory of our family, but also our community, and our nation. As you read this letter from God to His sons, pray for the men you listed above.

From: God
To: My Son Whose Heart I am Knocking On

My Son,

I know you have been waiting on that introduction. The introduction of a Father talking to His son. You may or may not have heard it when you needed it, but it is here now. The wisdom of a Father to his boy is here. Why? Because you are no longer a boy, but a man. And good fathers give sound wisdom to the man their son is becoming. So, listen to My words, and take heed to the instructions I am giving you.

Son, I love you. I see you now, and have always seen you. I see the strength in you coming alive. I see the way you make decisions and lead the people in your life. You are doing the best you can to make great decisions for those you love. Now, I need you to make godly decisions for the ones you love. The difference between a great decision and a godly decision is that in a godly decision, you invite Me, Your Heavenly Father in to help you do what is right. It has benefits right now, and into eternity. When you simply make what you think is a great decision, good as it may be, it only has benefits for the here and now. I have made you for more than that.

My son, I love you. I have set so many eyes on you: your family, friends, neighbors, and even the eyes of your enemies are on you. What do they see? DO they see that you are My Son? DO they know that when they come to you, you will say what I always say, in the way I say it? Will they say of you, "He's just like his Father, GOD?" My Son, I want you to be identified as MY SON to any and everybody who comes in contact with you.

I have made My men to be hunters. When you or your family need food, YOU go out and find it. It is the same spiritually. You have spiritual hunger pains that you been trying to fill in good ways, but not God ways. So, I am sending you out on a hunt. Your tool? The Bible.

Go into the Bible to hunt for this spiritual food. Eat, digest, and let it nourish your soul:

Ephesians 4
John 3:16 (the whole book of John eventually)
Romans 10:9
Ephesians 5
Psalm 51
Psalm 91
Exodus 23:24-26
Ezekiel 36:2

Son, **I need you to repent from your rebellion.** *"I haven't done anything wrong? What did I do?"* My Son, **you've tried to get through life on your own strength, making your own decisions, and doing it your own way.** You need Me, and I am here for YOU! Accept Me in your heart, and let Me be your Lord (owner – chief – leader - decision maker – friend - Father) and let Me be your Savior (eternal security of peace after life on earth).

I have been knocking on your heart with everything you need. Let me in. I will train, guide, and protect you in all your ways, and make you strong enough for yourself and your family. Your family doesn't just want a good husband and father, they want a GODLY husband and father. It is impossible to love them the way they need you to love them without Me. But with ME, you can do anything! Just ask Me, son. I will answer and teach you. Are you breathing? Then it is not too late.

My Son, who do YOU see when you see yourself? DO you see yourself as My son? If not, today is the day to make that change. The hour is late, and I am coming back soon. I bring My sons with Me, but My enemies will have no place with Me.

"Behold, I stand at the door, and knock: if any man hear my voice, and open the door, I will come in to him, and will sup with him, and he with me." Revelation 3:20 (KJV)

Let Jesus into your heart. He is knocking. Let Him in.

Love, Your Heavenly Father

Respond

What is the in-between of this letter? (Focus)

_____

_____

_____

_____

_____

_____

What is God saying about Himself? (Perspective)

_____

_____

_____

_____

_____

What is God saying about me? (Perspective)

_____

_____

_____

_____

_____

What advice is God giving me to live victoriously in this in-between? (Action)

_____

_____

_____

_____

_____

PART 4

As God worked on my heart through His letters to me, He eventually allowed me the opportunity to start sharing. Now, this sharing did not come while I was in the thick of it; I had to come to a place of peace in my soul, and be in a position that the Word was working for me.

My dearest friend and sister in the faith, NaTeesha, told me one day, "Jerrica, when it comes to seeing lives transformed through your testimony, you have to live it, then give it." Her words could not be truer. If there's one thing that years of working with children has taught me, they can smell a phony…and they usually call them out.

One day, my sister and I went to a women's retreat for the weekend. If you know us, you know that was so far out of our comfort zone. However, we went anyway. As I was preparing for the trip, I felt an urge to print the letters and turn them into bookmarks. I had about 20 or so letters at that point, so I took each letter, formatted it into two columns and printed them. Then I folded them in half, and put index cards in the middle for women to respond to what they were hearing from God as they read the encouragement. I packed them in my bag and said nothing about them.

When we reached the location, I showed my friend the bookmarks, and asked if it was okay for me to give them out. She strongly encouraged that if God led me to do it, ABSOLUTELY! The weekend went on, and it was our last day. We reached the conference room at the closing session; I had the bookmarks in tow, and was full of fear. "*What if the retreat host feels I am overstepping and gets mad at me?*" rang in my ears. NaTeesha glanced at me and asked if I was ready. I shook my head, but she raised her hand and told the group that I had a gift to give everyone. I was about to pass out on the floor, but the retreat hostess welcomed the idea.

Filled with fear, I stood up and explained the bookmarks, and how God downloaded them on my heart. My friend suggested that each person pick their own instead of me passing them out, so I walked around the room and had the ladies pick one. Crazy enough, there were exactly the right amount for the women who were present! As I took my seat, one woman exclaimed, "Oh my God, Oh my God! This is the confirmation I needed!" The retreat host asked her to read it aloud, so she did. Humbled and nervous, I sat and heard what she read. First, I was floored at what God said, because I didn't remember writing those words. I was even more astounded that God used me as His scribe and allowed me to pen what this woman needed. The next thing that happened brought tears to my eyes.

The retreat host instructed everyone to read their bookmark, and take in what The Lord was saying to them. What followed next was a soft chorus of, "Mmm," and "Wow," as the ladies read. I sat with my head down, crying. One by one, the women slowly read God's heart to them through tears, all declaring it was exactly what they needed, and was confirmation for something God had been dealing with in them. When everyone was finished reading, NaTeesha turned to me. "I am proud of you," she said. My heart felt so full.

Having seen the power of God through my obedience to share what He penned on my heart, I pondered. *What if I could share this with others? What other things are on my heart that could reach others?* I decided at that moment to start a blog. Keep in mind, God had already told me, "It is not a bookmark, it is a book." So, at the cusp of making the blog, God sweetly reiterated, "It's not a blog, it's a book." I - in true Jerrica fashion, went forward creating my blog, anyway. Because God knows that was the progression I needed to release the fear of writing a book, He allowed it, but left the reminder on the table for when I would follow through.

I will discuss more about the blog in the next section of the book; however, here is a snippet of the ponderings that surfaced as I sought to provide, "Exhortation for the mature, instruction for the growing, and encouragement for all."

POINTS TO PONDER

From: God
To: The One with the Yeast Infection

My Beloved,

You love the taste of food, and eating. But your taste buds have been deceived. You are enjoying the bread that does not give life, but takes it away. You are consuming the bread that you have worked for, instead of what is being freely given. You are enjoying the bread that takes your energy and leaves you ready to sleep; it slows you down. You have been eating the yeast rolls of the bread of the Pharisees - you My beloved, have a yeast infection.

Similar to seeds that fall on thorny ground, the yeast infected heart is excited to hear; however, it's filled with half-truths and lies, because of what it takes in. Drained, it chokes the life out of the truth instead of receiving it. You need a yeast-free life, which comes from submitting to a yeast-free Bread.

First, your taste buds must change. The words of affirmation and who you seek them from must change. Your source of fulfillment and direction must change. Comparing yourself to the world and even believers must change. Your heart must transition from that which causes condemnation and stagnancy, to being compelled to righteousness and reaping- the results of the yeast-free life.

My Son says in John 6:35 (NIV), "Then Jesus declared, 'I am the bread of life. Whoever comes to me will never go hungry, and whoever believes in me will never be thirsty.'"

Are you hungry for True Bread, sealed by My approval, authentically owned by Me? You know True Bread because when you eat it, it gives you energy to DO the things I am calling you to do. It is enough, lasts, and fills you. True Bread makes you come alive! Once you eat it, you come back for more because it fuels you better than a cup of coffee. True Bread sustains you.

To be sustained is to be girded up and stabilized. When you are sustained, you are not rocked to your core when pressures arise. True Bread has a smell that draws you to leave what you thought you know, to follow what is true. When you taste the Bread of Heaven, you will never want to bread of the Pharisees ever again. Why? Because you will never hunger again.

True Bread is available to you today. Just come. When you come nearer, I draw nearer. It is a promise in My word. "Come near to God and he will come near to you. Wash your hands, you sinners, and purify your hearts, you double-minded." (James 4:8 KJV)

True Bread washes, purifies, and removes all barriers that causes you not to come. So, come. If it does not look, smell, feel, taste, or sound like Jesus – it's because it isn't Him. Don't let works or the yeast of the lost slip you up, thinking of all the prerequisites to a holy life. Come to Jesus intimately, loving, obeying, and doing what He says over and over again. Be what you feed on. It will fill you.

Love, Abba Father

Respond

What is the in-between of this letter? (Focus)

_____
_____
_____
_____
_____
_____

What is God saying about Himself? (Perspective)

_____
_____
_____
_____
_____
_____

What is God saying about me? (Perspective)

_____
_____
_____
_____
_____
_____

What advice is God giving me to live victoriously in this in-between?
(Action)

_____
_____
_____
_____
_____
_____

Exhausting God

You exhausted God? Wow! How did you do it? What did you say? When did He quit? You seriously learned all there was to learn about John 3:16? You've fully mastered the exegesis of Psalm 23? Whoa, that's wild! You **exhausted** GOD!

Definition of exhaust:

1. Drain (someone) of their physical or mental resources; tire out.

2. Use up (resources or reserves) completely.

Google Dictionary

Now this is a conversation we would likely never hear aloud, but how many of us think this in our hearts? How many of us (myself included), have been to a point where you can quote John 3:16 - King James Version, New International Version, and even the Message translations of the Bible, in your sleep? We believe we have a FULL grasp of EXACTLY what God meant in the verse and know all there is to know about all things John 3:16, but if one more preacher tries to throw their new spin on it, we are going to throw a fit!

This was me in March of 2019. I thought I had exhausted God, or at least a piece of what He said. I was sitting in the most fruitful Bible Study I'd ever attended to date, called, *Adorning His Bride*. As the teacher walked the class through the book of John, the Holy Spirit highlighted some attributes about Jesus. The assignment was to pick one attribute, and get to know Jesus in that way. Haphazardly, in genuine excitement I chose to learn Jesus as *The Bread of Life*. (John 6:25-56). It is lengthy, so I recommend you grab your Bible and take a look.

One excerpt that stood out to me was John 6:26-27, 35 (NIV):

[26]"Jesus answered, 'Very truly I tell you, you are looking for me, not because you saw the signs I performed but because you ate the loaves and had your fill. [27] Do not work for food that spoils, but for food that endures to eternal life, which the Son of Man will give you. For on him God the Father has placed his seal of approval." [35] Then Jesus declared, "I am the bread of life. Whoever comes to me will never go hungry, and whoever believes in me will never be thirsty.'"

Initially, I saw the scripture like, "Ok, you are the Bread of Life. Cool." But once I took it slowly, (https://refreshhercourse.blog/2019/11/13/take-it-slow/) my heart naturally did something I had long desired it would do: I questioned God. Yes, I asked God a question! "God, what did Jesus mean when he said, 'For on him God the Father has placed his seal of approval' in verse 27? In Jesus' day, did bread have a stamp of approval?" This is when the levy broke! I researched the phrase, **Bible times, bread, stamp,** and learned that back then, bakers made bread in the town's community ovens. So each baker could identify his own loaves, he marked the bread with a stamp so everyone knew it was his. That mark proved the authenticity of the loaf, its owner, and proved the quality of ingredients was what the baker said they were. MIND BLOWN! Jesus unfolded a revelation about His authenticity so deep, I could barely catch my breath!

After this, I researched all the related verses to wrap my heart around learning that Jesus was the True Bread! I was ecstatic! The next week in Bible study, I reported what Jesus revealed about Himself as the others did. Afterwards, I was ready to pick the next attribute, because I had successfully exhausted God…or so I thought! Our teacher said, "The Holy Spirt is instructing me to tell us to stay with the attribute you picked to learn Jesus, and DO NOT MOVE FROM IT." My heart SANK! I was a knowledge addict, and I wanted to get a new attribute. The war in my heart must have been obvious, because the teacher called me out. She said she knew it would be hard for me because I thought I exhausted God, but "STAY THERE!"

At home, I surrendered my little heart and repented for thinking I exhausted the inexhaustible God, and crawled into His presence, ready to hear. Almost as SOON as I postured my heart to listen, more questions came. During the remaining four weeks, as I SOUGHT THE HEART of God and not just empty information, I learned:

- The difference between leavened and unleavened bread.
- The process of making unleavened bread.
- I MADE unleavened bread that we ate for communion during Bible study one week! It had a WHOLE NEW MEANING.
- Songs that I used to love that spoke of Jesus as the Living Bread came alive in a new way in my heart.
- Bread-related scriptures from the old and new testaments jumped off the pages.

- I learned that bread is a staple food in every culture.
- I learned the definitions of bread, yeast, and the like.
- I received a prophetic exhortation regarding Jesus being the Bread of Life for me.
- God gave me a song that I sang for weeks in Bible study; others were blessed by it. (Go, JESUS!)

All of this came because I DID NOT exhaust God. If I go back RIGHT NOW to John 6, I am assured that something new and useable would grip my heart and change me. You see sis, the day I stopped thinking I exhausted God, was the day I fell deeper in love with Him. And that love is still deepening in my heart and changing the way I live my life. He wants that for you, too!

Go back to the attribute or scripture you thought you exhausted the life out of, and don't move from it unless God tells you to. Stay, rest your heart there, and allow it to take true interest. And, ASK QUESTIONS. God will faithfully answer them if you want to know HIM.

Here are a few passages I'm SLOWLY revisiting. Maybe they will be a good place for you to start, too:

- 1 Peter 1:13-2:3
- 1 Peter 1:3-11
- Galatians 5:16-26
- 1 John 1:5-7

Selah...

Respond

What is the in-between of this letter? (Focus)

_____
_____
_____
_____
_____
_____

What is God saying about Himself? (Perspective)

_____
_____
_____
_____
_____
_____

What is God saying about me? (Perspective)

_____
_____
_____
_____
_____
_____

What advice is God giving me to live victoriously in this in-between? (Action)

_____
_____
_____
_____
_____
_____

Living Water, Dirty Glass

I do not know many people who'd walk into a restaurant and say, "I'll have a lemonade, dirty glass please." You could imagine the look on your dinner guests, the server, and any onlooker's faces, looking at you like, *Did they just order what I think they ordered?* You can also imagine all eyes on you as the server brings you the glass and a straw, watching intensely in disbelief as you lift the cup and drink from a dirty glass.

The average person would deem it socially unacceptable to drink from a dirty glass. Why then, do we expect folks to experience the thirst quenching goodness of Jesus Christ from our lives, if we ourselves are a *dirty glass*? Let me expound.

In Matthew 23:25-26, Jesus is addressing a group of people who know the Word of God. They can quote scripture left and right, and have it committed to memory. These are the people who will quickly check you if you misquote a verse, skirt isn't long enough, or they feel your spirit doesn't check all the boxes to their standards. Yet, these same people will give you the death glare if you sit in their seat in church or cut them off in the parking lot; they'll cuss you out if take them *out of their religion*. Now I'm sure by now you are in the *amen corner*, whispering to yourself all the reasons to justifying why you don't go to church, convincing yourself that you're on a personal journey with God. Pause one second - the verse states:

25 "Woe to you, teachers of the law and Pharisees, you hypocrites! You clean the outside of the cup and dish, but inside they are full of greed and self-indulgence. 26 Blind Pharisee! First clean the inside of the cup and dish, and then the outside also will be clean."

Matthew 23:25-26 (KJV)

Beloved, you and I are not above rebuke if there's any greed and self-indulgence on the throne of our hearts. God wants us to focus our time and efforts on being clean on the inside; the outside will take care of itself. Inwardly, I used to have a very bad habit of complaining about work, singleness, how people wronged me, and the like. It felt good to unload my complaints on whomever would listen. And I felt justified when they affirmed my broken thinking, saying, "You are right, they did you wrong! I'd be upset, too!" It almost felt like a chemical release of joy when my complaints were affirmed. BUT, when I complained in one breath and tried telling someone about the goodness of Jesus Christ in the next, they couldn't receive it. Why? Because **I was pouring Living Water from a dirty glass, tainting it with a broken perspective.** It saddened me that I couldn't get through to my friends about the love of God because I complained too much. Simple answer, stop complaining, right? Wrong. I had to change my heart towards my circumstances. I needed Jesus to give me the mind of Christ.

"He was oppressed and afflicted, yet he did not open his mouth; he was led like a lamb to the slaughter, and as a sheep before its shearers is silent, so he did not open his mouth."

Isaiah 53:7 (NIV)

2 Corinthians 4:7-11 New International Version (NIV)

⁷ "But we have this treasure in jars of clay to show that this all-surpassing power is from God and not from us. ⁸ We are hard pressed on every side, but not crushed; perplexed, but not in despair; ⁹ persecuted, but not abandoned; struck down, but not destroyed. ¹⁰ We always carry around in our body the death of Jesus, so that the life of Jesus may also be revealed in our body. ¹¹ For we who are alive are always being given over to death for Jesus' sake, so that his life may also be revealed in our mortal body."

Philippians 2:5-11 King James Version (KJV)

⁵ "Let this mind be in you, which was also in Christ Jesus.

⁶ Who, being in the form of God, thought it not robbery to be equal with God.

⁷ But made himself of no reputation, and took upon him the form of a servant, and was made in the likeness of men:

⁸ And being found in fashion as a man, he humbled himself, and became obedient unto death, even the death of the cross.

⁹ Wherefore God also hath highly exalted him, and given him a name which is above every name:

¹⁰ That at the name of Jesus every knee should bow, of things in heaven, and things in earth, and things under the earth;

¹¹ And that every tongue should confess that Jesus Christ is Lord, to the glory of God the Father."

In a nutshell, **I had to go LOW and thrive there.** To endure **trials like a good soldier.** I had to start letting God give me His heart, allowing Him to make me more like Him in the way I thought and spoke and responded to adversity. **This dying allowed me to truly "Count it all joy when you fall into diverse temptations."** (James 1:2-3). *As I cleaned myself on the inside, authentic words of life poured from me, and those who heard, felt them. Listeners* *became doers of the same Living Water (Word) that transformed the inside of me, because they saw it really transformed me from the inside.* Over time, people saw the pretty package on the outside matched what's on the inside of me. They were able to receive what I poured, and their thirst for truth was quenched.

When was the last time you cleaned the inside of your cup? Today is a good day to start. God wants to use you to your maximum potential. He won't serve Himself out of you, if you're not a clean vessel. Let Him clean that area that only you and Him know about.

"If we confess our sins, he is faithful and just and will forgive us our sins and **purify us from all unrighteousness."**

1 John 1:9 (NIV)

Respond

What is the in-between of this letter? (Focus)

_____

_____

_____

_____

_____

What is God saying about Himself? (Perspective)

_____

_____

_____

_____

_____

What is God saying about me? (Perspective)

_____

_____

_____

_____

_____

What advice is God giving me to live victoriously in this in-between? (Action)

_____

_____

_____

_____

_____

Good Grief

Have you ever been so frustrated and bothered in your spirit by an act against God by yourself or others that you could scream, or cry? I have been there so many times. I believe that every true follower of Christ has been there at some point in time. In my fervor, I recall praying a prayer that changed everything. "Lord, break my heart with the things that break Your heart."

Initially reading this prayer, you may be thinking, "What is wrong with that? You wanted to feel what God felt, so you could pray." True, yes. However, I will confess that I wasn't ready for God's answer to my prayer. I was a teenager and I was on fire for Jesus Christ. I loved Him so much, I couldn't hold a conversation without mentioning Him. This wasn't some mission to convert others; there was a well springing up inside of me that I literally couldn't keep quiet. As I matured more in Jesus Christ, I learned about prayer and intercession - praying on other's behalf. This is where deep conviction gripped me. I wanted to pray more effective prayers with understanding, so I prayed the prayer I mentioned earlier, and BAM! I was so crushed and broken, y'all! Everything I saw grieved me. Not just things about others, things about ME! It felt like scales had fallen off my eyes and plugs came out my ears.

I heard my peers' conversations, and immediately got a sick feeling in my gut like I could throw up, because God was so offended with their vulgarity. At the time, I was wrestling with a particular sin that God wanted me free from. When I indulged in the sin rather than fighting it, I literally felt like God would remove His Spirit from me, and I would die! I grew to fear Him. When I saw behaviors of professing followers of Christ in their own spaces and how it was unlike what I saw of them in church, I could barely stand it. In my private time with God, I cried, and cried some more. It wasn't out of judgement, I asked God for mercy. I wanted our eyes and ears to be opened, so we'd stop making God angry by re-nailing His Son to the cross. I wanted us free!

Eventually, I asked God to relieve the weight, because I wouldn't survive under the grief He bears looking on unrepentant children. "Will you keep the fervor in my intercession, but lift the pain?" I asked Him. "Thank You for Jesus Christ, who bore it for us. Help us to realize that and change." God did it. At that moment, I had a whole new outlook on the weight of sin Jesus took for US on

Calvary. It deepened my love for Him so much, and still does.

What grieves you so much that it makes you change, pray (for real), and even speak up under direction of the Holy Spirit? I believe in *good grief*, which can also be called conviction. Conviction is defined as "a firmly held belief or opinion." (Google Dictionary). What belief do you hold so firmly in Christ that it compels action? Let's look at a few examples:

16 "While Paul was waiting for them in Athens, he was greatly distressed to see that the city was full of idols. 17 So he reasoned in the synagogue with both Jews and God-fearing Greeks, as well as in the marketplace day by day with those who happened to be there." Acts 17:16-17 (NIV)

Here, Apostle Paul had made a trip to Athens to share the Gospel of Jesus Christ, and was greatly distressed, because the city was full of idols. Paul was experiencing *good grief.* It was conviction and grief that caused him to reason. Let's look at another example:

19 "A number who had practiced sorcery brought their scrolls together and burned them publicly. When they calculated the value of the scrolls, the total came to fifty thousand drachmas." Acts 19:19 (NIV)

Here, former magicians who had come to the knowledge of Christ Jesus felt good grief, and conviction about the life they decided to change. They burned up the very thing that offended Holy God, not caring about the cost. Let's see our last example:

3 "They said to me, "Those who survived the exile and are back in the province are in great trouble and disgrace. The wall of Jerusalem is broken down, and its gates have been burned with fire." 4 When I heard these things, I sat down and wept. For some days I mourned and fasted and prayed before the God of heaven. 5 and I answered the king, "If it pleases the king and if your servant has found favor in his sight, let him send me to the city in Judah where my ancestors are buried so that I can rebuild it." Nehemiah 1:3-4, 2:5 (NIV)

Nehemiah was a cupbearer for the king who feared God, and brought news that his city was without walls, protection, and open for the enemy to siege it. This deeply grieved him; however, it was good grief. So, Nehemiah prayerfully and bravely asked the king for permission to rebuild the walls of the city. He could not stay still. What I loved most was his pattern before action. "*I sat down, and wept. For some days I mourned and fasted, and prayed before the God of heaven.*" He did not go rouge, sisters! Chaka Khan lied - we are NOT every woman, it is NOT all in us. If GOD does not breathe on our pursuit of righteousness, it is self-righteousness. If we go rouge, remedying our good grief ourselves, we take the good out of it.

Summary

All of us who are in Christ will experience grief. What makes it good grief is if we are compelled in our hearts to change and act with Jesus in it. Nehemiah gives us a way to go to God with our good grief:

1. Sit down.
2. Weep.
3. Mourn.
4. Fast.
5. Pray.
6. Ask in faith.
7. Go in faith.

Again I ask, what grieves you so much that it makes you change, pray (for real), and even speak up under direction of the Holy Spirit?

Respond

What is the in-between of this letter? (Focus)

_____
_____
_____
_____
_____

What is God saying about Himself? (Perspective)

_____
_____
_____
_____
_____

What is God saying about me? (Perspective)

_____
_____
_____
_____
_____

What advice is God giving me to live victoriously in this in-between?
(Action)

_____
_____
_____
_____
_____

PART 5
REFRESH HER COURSE

"It's not a bookmark, it's a book. It's not a blog, it's a book," God reminded me kindly. Blogging what He shared with me was easy. I didn't have to think too much and saw wonderful wins, but I knew in my heart I wasn't being fully obedient due to fear. I was afraid of the unknown, success, and failure. What if I got teased and embarrassed by the things I shared being taken out of context? Was I ready for all that comes with transparency and sharing truth with a degenerate yet desperate world starving for real love?

Where are you right now? What is the *in-between* that that caused you to pick up this book? Write about it below.

_____
_____
_____
_____
_____
_____
_____
_____
_____
_____
_____

_____

_____

_____

_____

_____

_____

_____

_____

_____

_____

_____

_____

_____

_____

How has God spoken to your *in-between* already?

_____

_____

_____

_____

_____

_____

_____

_____

_____

_____

_____

I sensed that other women would need the direction and guidance you are describing. That's why I released the *Refresh Her Course* blog. I wanted women to see my process, which can simply be described as:

1. Cry out to God.
2. Expectantly wait for His answer to your cry.
3. Write down what He says.
4. Meditate on what He says.
5. Implement what He says.
6. Thank Him for the change He made in your perspective and situation.

It was not rocket science, I just had to do it. If you were very honest with yourself, have you really put into play what God has already instructed you to do to change your mindset and/or your situation? Circle one.

Yes/ No

God was looking for more than commitment from me - He wanted me to surrender. By committing to His plan for my *in-between*, I was saying, "Okay, God. I will get behind this plan and see how it works out." But by surrendering to His plan, I'm saying, "Lord, You have control in every area of my life. I come under Your control, and submit myself to Your plan for my *in-between*. With commitment, the control is in my hand, and I can jump ship at any given time. With surrender to The Lord, all control is on Him; cooperation is my only goal. It shows Him whether challenge or smooth sailing, whatever character-building lessons come my way, He is the teacher and I am the student, not the other way around. When navigating the *in-between*, Jesus Christ needs to be at the head of our hearts, and we must willingly submit to follow through on what our loving Creator allows.

Have you been in a place of commitment or surrender? How do you know?

_____

_____

_____

_____

_____

_____

_____

_____

_____

_____

_____

_____

If you have been in a place of commitment, what have you read in this book or heard from the Lord that encourages you to move into surrender?

_____

_____

_____

_____

_____

_____

_____

_____

_____

_____

_____

The Blog Pt. 2

The following blogs were some of the heavy-hitters that really shaped my surrender to God to navigate His plan for my *in-between* places. I was *in-between*:

- Contentment and despair.
- Freedom and bondage.
- Joy and pain.
- Where I was, and where I wanted to be.

And the list goes on. What's your current *in-between*?

_____

_____

_____

_____

_____

_____

Enjoy the following exhortations and encouragements and remember to respond to what God is saying to you through them. Your response is not a debate with God, but a reflection of what you hear, and the actions He's encouraging you to follow. Throwing a *thank you* in there doesn't hurt, either.

I Think I Figured out Who I'm Talking to...

So, our amazing God puts ministry right in front of you when you don't even realize it. He recently reconnected me with someone I didn't expect to hit it off with. She is a kind person, but can be misunderstood, and has a lot of room to grow, but don't we all? There are a couple of things about her that I see in myself:

- [ ] She is a believer in Christ.
- [ ] She has been churched.
- [ ] She is currently unchurched/under-churched.
- [ ] But she wants to do better is seeing her deep need for God.
- [ ] She is slowly pursuing God and starting somewhere.
- [ ] She is reading the Bible.
- [ ] She wants to grow in understanding.

So as you see, we have a lot in common. When I think about the people God puts in my life to encourage, they generally have a similar makeup:

- Churched.
- Love God.
- Unchurched.
- Wanting Him.
- Seeking Him more.

I believe this is the woman who Refresh Her Course blog is for. This blog is to encourage the woman who is over performance, and desires the person of God. It is for the woman who wants to take it seriously and wants to take it personal. It is for the woman who tried the world, tried God and is wise enough to acknowledge that God is better. It is for the woman who is ready to die to self to be alive in Christ Jesus. It is for YOU. It is for me. So yes, I want to exhort (urgently stir) the mature in Christ who know better, and are consistently pressing for it. The ones who are not satisfied with being in the same place with God this time next year, will grow so much more. I am instructing the woman who is growing in her faith, sharing what the Holy Spirit says and the things I KNOW work because I tried them. Even if I've been slow to exercise them, I know they work because I have seen others work the principle and get results. I am writing to all who need a drink from the flowing stream of God's abundant encouragement. I am called to refresh others and make streams. The verse that really came to me when thinking about this blog is:

5Blessed are those whose strength is in you, whose hearts are set on pilgrimage. 6As they pass through the Valley of Baca, they make it a place of springs; even the autumn rain covers it with pools. 7They go from strength to strength, until each appears before God in Zion.

Psalm 84:5-7 (NIV)

God has given me encouragement in the valley of weeping that has refreshed me, and is carrying me through until I get to Him. I am called to do the same: Encourage women in the valley and refresh her, giving her strength until she reaches Jesus.

Thank You Lord, for showing me who I am talking to. May I speak so only You are heard.

Respond

What is the in-between of this letter? (Focus)

_____

_____

_____

_____

_____

_____

What is God saying about Himself? (Perspective)

_____

_____

_____

_____

_____

_____

What is God saying about me? (Perspective)

_____

_____

_____

_____

_____

_____

What advice is God giving me to live victoriously in this in-between? (Action)

_____

_____

_____

_____

_____

_____

What If He Does?

Girrrrrllllll! Ok, we are jumping straight into the Word on this one! God's here with me this morning!

God dropped an encouraging revelation on me last night. I'll be honest with you, I was discouraged, longing, and feeding my soul the enemy's lies. He was winning ground in my heart. The seeds God had sown were being snatched as quickly as they were thrown, until...

"That same day Jesus went out of the house and sat by the lake. ²Such large crowds gathered around him that he got into a boat and sat in it, while all the people stood on the shore. ³Then he told them many things in parables, saying: "A farmer went out to sow his seed. ⁴As he was scattering the seed, some fell along the path, and the birds came and ate it up. ⁵Some fell on rocky places, where it did not have much soil. It sprang up quickly, because the soil was shallow. ⁶But when the sun came up, the plants were scorched, and they withered because they had no root. ⁷Other seed fell among thorns, which grew up and choked the plants. ⁸Still other seed fell on good soil, where it produced a crop—a hundred, sixty or thirty times what was sown. ⁹Whoever has ears, let them hear.""

Matthew 13:1-9 (NIV)

My struggle to believe the things of God because of the culprit that was coming to take the seed of truth that was being spread over my heart came rushing back. FOR YEARS, I couldn't figure out why I wasn't victorious in this area. *My heart IS good ground, but why are these things happening that are keeping my maturity stagnant?* God started breaking down this passage more:

¹⁸ *"Listen then to what the parable of the sower means: ¹⁹ When anyone hears the message about the kingdom and does not understand it, the evil one comes and snatches away what was sown in their heart. This is the seed sown along the path. ²⁰ The seed falling on rocky ground refers to someone who hears the word and at once receives it with joy. ²¹ But since they have no root, they last only a short time. When trouble or persecution comes because of the word, they quickly fall away. ²² The seed falling among the thorns refers to someone who hears the word, but the worries of this life and the deceitfulness of wealth choke the word, making it unfruitful. ²³ But the seed falling on good soil refers to someone who hears the word and understands it. This is the one who produces a crop, yielding a hundred, sixty or thirty times what was sown."*

Matthew 13:18-23 (NIV)

Heart Posture	Seed Outcome
seed sown along the path	Hears the message about the Kingdom, and does not understand it. The evil one comes and snatches away what was sown in their heart.
rocky ground	Someone who hears the Word and at once receives it with joy. But since they have no root, they last only a short time. When trouble or persecution comes because of the Word, they quickly fall away.
thorns	Someone who hears the Word, but the worries about life and the deceitfulness of wealth, choke the Word, making it unfruitful.
good soil	Someone who hears the Word and understands it. This is the one who produces a crop, yielding one hundred, sixty or thirty times what was sown.

Do you get it? Everyone's heart is one of these four at some point. I was floating between the path, thorny, and good. It was seasonal, but seasonal wasn't good enough for me...I wanted eternal. My desire is to have my heart be eternally *good soil*, to not only receive and understand God's Word, but YIELED LASTING FRUIT! Do you want that, too? Keep reading a little more.

So one day, I was talking to my *Elizabeth*, who refused to let me get off the phone downcast, when we KNOW how good God is! Then she said something that snatched the seed right back out of the enemy's hand and loosed me from the grip of the thorns that were trying to choke life out of me: **"But what if He do?"**

So now I ask you:

- I know the enemy told you that God may not make you a wife after all these years, **"But what if He does?"**
- I know the enemy said God will not make you a mother and your womb cannot hold babies, **"But what if He does?"**
- I know God healed you once before and it lasted for a little bit, but the issues came back and what if He don't, **"But what if He does?"**
- I know your parents didn't say *I love you* and it made you feel so unlovable that even God can't love you, **"But what if He does?"**
- I know people said your testimony wasn't dramatic enough and God can't possibly use it to change a generation, **"But what if He does?"**
- I know your family is all jacked up and has always been jacked up, and the enemy tells you God can't restore them, **"But what if He does?"**
- I know you may not think you're the bravest, boldest, prettiest, speak well and have doubted if God can use YOU for His glory, BUT WHAT IF HE DOES?

"What if He does," KILLS doubt, but "What if He doesn't," builds doubt!

YOU have to get indignant with the devil and let him know, SO WHAT about all you are telling me God will NOT do for me, through me, with me, BUT WHAT IF HE DO? What if He does make a miracle out of all the emergencies in my life? What if He does give me a new song that I can't contain, and even though I am no songbird by MAN'S standards, the song of praise in me will restore my heart and other's hope? What if He DOES heal my sickly child? What if He DOES do it all?

1 John 5:14-15 (KJV)

[14] And **this** is **the confidence that we have in him**, that, if we ask **any thing** according **to his will, he heareth us:**

[15] And **if we know** that he hear us, **whatsoever we ask, we know** that we have the petitions that we desired of him.

CHANGE THE GAME, SIS! Kill doubt in your heart once and for all. For every time the enemy says, "What if He don't," HIT back with, "BUT WHAT IF HE DO?" Then praise God for WHO HE IS!

WONDERFUL COUNSELOR

MIGHTY GOD
EVERLASTING FATHER
PRINCE OF PEACE
LOVER OF YOUR SOUL
GOOD SHEPHERD
AND THE LIST GOES ON!!!!

Get a song in your heart and a praise on your lips! Do it NOW! Break the hold of the thorn NOW!

Someone asked me yesterday, "Why do you love Jesus?" My response was, "I just do. He saved me from death, even suicide." Girl, the way I told it, I didn't even convince myself! But after God restored and led me into all truth, I emphatically declare, I love Jesus because every time the world tried to kill me, HE FOUGHT FOR ME! Every time the enemy tries to make me doubt what God can't or won't do in my life, GOD FIGHTS FOR ME. He always fights for me, and for that, I LOVE HIM! He has moved mountains to pursue my heart! He has given nations to have ME! I love Him because He first loved ME! He loves you too Sis, and wants YOU to be free! He wants to use you for His glory and give you a life that impacts the world for His glory. I know the enemy just shot that arrow of, "What if He don't," but I QUENCH it by lifting the Shield of Faith and say to you, "But what if He do?"

Respond

What is the in-between of this letter? (Focus)

_____

_____

_____

_____

_____

_____

What is God saying about Himself? (Perspective)

_____

_____

_____

_____

_____

_____

What is God saying about me? (Perspective)

_____

_____

_____

_____

_____

_____

What advice is God giving me to live victoriously in this in-between?
(Action)

_____

_____

_____

_____

_____

_____

The Waiting Game

God loves us so much! It would do this encouragement injustice to not provide some background. This past weekend, I rode the struggle bus and my house showed it! My mother always tells me, "The condition of your house reveals the condition of your mind." Basically, she was saying if your mind's junky and messy, it will start to show in your home. Boy oh boy, did it show in mine! Work had been occupying the better part of my LIFE week, lol. I felt I had no time at all to clean my house, let alone my mind. I was discouraged.

I'm sure I'm not the only one who can't relax enough to sense the presence and voice of God if my house is a mess. It seems like it makes me more emotional, because I want to sense and enjoy the time I spend with Him. But when the house and my mind are cluttered, it's rough. I can hear some of y'all saying, "Well just clean up!" If it was that easy, I would've already done it. Fast forward to the end of this testimony: It WAS that easy. Over the course of a weekend, God encouraged my soul, which gave me strength and a jolt to clean up. Then, He invited me to play a game...the waiting game.

I was in the midst of cleaning and organizing my dresser when my *Elizabeth* called and said the Holy Spirit dropped one hot off the press! OF COURSE I was ready to hear whatever the Holy Spirit had to say; she invited me (and I am inviting YOU) to play the waiting game! This is what she shared:

The Waiting Game

If you want to successfully wait for the fullness of God in your life, you have to totally redefine in your heart what waiting is and how to do it. God's not having us wait just for cars, houses, husbands, babies, healings and help. He wants us to wait with faithful hearts for the second coming of His Son, Jesus Christ. He wants to know in all forms of waiting, we will remain in Him, obedient and full of hope, even if TIME maxes out on our self-created timeline. TIME is a system God created to develop us into the children He desires us to be. TIME is a gift.

A part of the gift of time is waiting. Waiting is as hard as you make it, but God has given US encouragement TODAY regarding HOW to wait WELL! These are the steps to playing The Waiting Game:

- Listen to others' testimonies. In Hebrews 11, our goal is to gain a great testimony. Revelations 12:11 (KJV) says, "And they overcame him by the blood of the Lamb, and by the word of their testimony; and they loved not their lives unto the death." Testimony helps us overcome! Hebrews 11 shows us TRUE testimonies regarding suffering well. FLOOD yourself with true testimony!

- Seek God desperately! First, define what it means to *seek*. Learn where to look for God! The world tells us to look high, but the WORD tells us to look low.

Seeking God desperately shows us three things:

1. His characteristics.
2. His location.
3. His command.

Learn His characteristics, so you're not confused what He looks like.

My Elizabeth

Next, once you learn God's characteristics, location, and command:

- Meditate on His command day and night (Joshua 1:8). We have to consume the command like we do food. I eat morning, noon, and night, and even a few snacks. When we consume the command, we are abiding in Him and His Word in us (John 15:7).
- Practice! If we want a new perspective on waiting, we need an understanding of the vocabulary. Define these words to start:

petition	gratitude
prayer	servitude
thanksgiving	humility
praise	goodness
blessing	kindness

- Learn the definitions of these words, then practice using them.
- Look for examples in the Word that define each word. Ask questions like, *Who in the Bible was in thanksgiving? What were they thankful for? How did they express it?*

This next part is the GAME CHANGER during your wait, **be encouraged by the challenge and GO FOR IT! You're a hearer and a DOER! #takethechallenge #goforit #Joshuaspirit**

- Rehearse the good more than the bad! (I'm famous for rehearsing the bad, but the buck stops here TODAY!) If you're going to rehearse anything, rehearse the testimonies of those who suffered well in their wait, and reflect on the victories God is giving you as you exercise truth!
- Don't tear yourself down! Be your biggest encourager! Be your biggest fan!

How do I continue winning in the waiting game and encourage myself?

Speak LIFE! We build ourselves by:

1. Giving thanks for the opportunity to exercise (waiting).

Acknowledge the victories! It shows God you are acknowledging His direction, and heeding opportunity. When we do this, He creates MORE opportunity!

My Elizabeth

Next, we are to:

- Celebrate your training exercise!
- Acknowledge Him in ALL things- this is your daily devotion.

Turn complaints into compliments!

- Ask Him to make you sensitive to His direction.

Summary

In the Waiting Game, we are to define, find examples, and DO. We must:

1. Learn how to praise (exercise it).
2. Absolutely always give thanks to God.

Sis, we can wait well! Stay focused; use tunnel vision during this season. Let's keep our eyes off of other people and have our gaze set on God. And when you feel like you're longsuffering, review these game instructions to see if you've perfected them. It helps us realize that God is never late. While we're playing the game, the point isn't just us waiting on God...God's waiting on us!

Quick little testimony...

I was at odds with a family member I loved. God ministered to me about being vulnerable with Him and others, so His love could change both of us. I was scared and stressed about it, but because God encouraged me, I wanted to obey. I asked, "What is vulnerability?" Then, I defined it. "God, can you show me folks in the Bible who were vulnerable with You? This is challenging for me, because I do not want to get hurt again. I really want to trust You in this and see the greatest outcome." I sought the Lord and His examples in scripture. Sure as my name is Jerrica, the opportunity to make things right and apologize arose. As fear crept in, I quickly obeyed God and didn't give backtalk or excuses. Glory to God, my apology was received and we moved forward in peace. I celebrated with my friend how God granted me peace through my obedience. So, you see? The peace was always available, but God was waiting for ME to suffer well through the discomfort, seek Him, and exercise the obedience! It works! I won The Waiting Game in that circumstance!

Be encouraged! Thank You, Jesus Christ for the revelation! #Godiswaitingonme

Respond

What is the in-between of this letter? (Focus)

_____
_____
_____
_____
_____
_____

What is God saying about Himself? (Perspective)

_____
_____
_____
_____
_____

What is God saying about me? (Perspective)

_____
_____
_____
_____
_____

What advice is God giving me to live victoriously in this in-between? (Action)

_____
_____
_____
_____
_____

Protect the In Between

Sis! God dropped this one just for me. I really hope it blesses you, though. First, I will provide some context:

- I'm a 28-year-old virgin.
- I've had ample opportunity to NOT be a 28-year-old virgin.
- I'm only a 28-year-old virgin because of the magnificent, unending, love and protection and correction of Almighty GOD.
- I have tried to get as close to the edge of my virginity without falling off the cliff. Thinking how far I went during some of those encounters left me broken, empty and disappointed in my lack of self-control. Until I had a revelation about my heart condition and what I needed God to deliver me from.
- The only good thing in me is Christ Jesus' Holy Spirit. HE is the reason I have not dragged my body through the dirt of an intimate union outside of the protection of marriage. HE is the reason why conviction strikes and repentance presents itself for me to change.
- It gets harder to crawl out of guilt and shame of where my thoughts sometimes go and my actions want to take me; however, repentance, the 180 degree turn from sin back to God with the mind to never turn back again is always the right option.
- And once more, I'm ONLY a virgin today because of the never-ending, all consuming, reckless love of GOD.

So how is that for background information? Now, on to the encouragement. The Holy Spirit is always on time, but sometimes, I'm a little late to the party. A few months ago, there was a morning when I was in the *fight of the month*. You know, ladies - that blessed fertility window fight. The window of time where one of the reasons why you were created reminds you that you are 100% woman, and 100% ready to function in your role….errrrrrrkkkkkk! It screeches the wheels of virginity, because you do not have a God-honoring outlet through marriage yet. So what now? You protect the in-between(s), of course.

There are four in-betweens that the Holy Spirit advised me to protect:

1. Protect what's between your eyes– your mind.

2. Protect what's between your chest– your heart.
3. Protect what's between your legs– your virtue.
4. Protect the space between where you are and where you desire to be.

Okay, this is the cliff hanger! Check the next post to see how the Holy Spirit spells these out for us.

Love ya!

Hear the message here:

Respond

What is the in-between of this letter? (Focus)

_____
_____
_____
_____
_____
_____

What is God saying about Himself? (Perspective)

_____
_____
_____
_____
_____
_____

What is God saying about me? (Perspective)

_____
_____
_____
_____
_____

What advice is God giving me to live victoriously in this in-between? (Action)

_____
_____
_____
_____
_____
_____

Conclusion

You have reached the end of the book. You've seen and reflected on the lessons God is showing you, and created an action plan based on His expert advice regarding how to navigate the in-between. But don't stop here! These lessons and what God has shown you through the journaling questions are what you need for the rest of your journey with Him. Keep pursuing Him! Keep surrendering to His love and correction. Embrace the *ouch*, *mmm*, and *ah-ha* moments as you navigate life with Jesus Christ. Don't ignore the Holy Spirit's invitation to stay a little longer, go a little deeper, and to take the narrow road.

As you reach the back cover; however, you may be wondering, *Jerrica, how do I know I am navigating the in-between successfully?* Here's how I can tell when I'm successfully navigating the in-between with God and not fainting - joyfully:

When I hold up the Word of God to the circumstances of my soul (mind, will, and emotions), have I moved from:
1. **Tumult**-- a loud, confused noise, especially one caused by a large mass of people; confusion or disorder. (Google definition) to **Peace**-- freedom from disturbance; a state or period in which there is no war or a war has ended. (Google definition)
2. **Argument**-- an exchange of diverging or opposite views, typically a heated or angry one. (Google definition) to **Agreement**-- the absence of incompatibility between two things; consistency; harmony or accordance in opinion or feeling. (Google definition)
3. **Angst**-- a feeling of deep anxiety or dread, typically an unfocused one about the human condition or the state of the world in general; a feeling of persistent worry about something trivial. (Google definition) to **Confidence**-- the feeling or belief that one can rely on someone or something; firm trust; the state of feeling certain about the truth of something. (Google Definition)
4. If the fist that I raised in foolishness, standing with the accuser unclenches into praise to our patient and loving God, willing to correct all who are willing to be corrected.

5. If the fist shook at my side in defense unclenches into surrender to the Way, the Truth, and the Life mapped out for me, even if I don't understand it all right now.

These are just some ways I gage how well I'm navigating the in-between with God. My heart prays and aches for you. My heart deeply desires that you simply put into practice casting your cares on the Lord, because His Word states that He cares for you (1 Peter 5:7). My heart desires that you endure these lessons in your youth on sticking with your first Love, turning from sin, controlling your mouth, preserving the right perspective of God. I want nothing less than for you to see **God** as the prize for not fainting, joyfully - not a man, baby, house, job, or business can squelch it.

If you do not remember anything else from this book, remember, the miracles are seen in simplicity. The voice of God is heard through constant communion. The journey is not given to the swift or the strong (Ecclesiastes. 9:11). Endure, Beloved.

Love, Abba's Daughter

ABOUT THE AUTHOR

Jerrica J. DeLaney is a daughter of the Most High God first, then a living epistle in her generation, shining light on the love of Jesus Christ, to inspire repentance and give hope to all who are in darkness. Jerrica's other works include, "The Best Five Minutes: A Prayer Journal for the Woman Unlearning Busy," and children's book, "Girl Power God's Way."

Made in the USA
Middletown, DE
28 October 2023

41432545R00104